Sexual Exploits Of A Nympho III

The Different Shades of Tina and Darren

By

Richard Jeanty

RJ Publication

Newark,

The characters and events in this book are fictitious. Any resemblance to actual persons, living or dead is purely coincidental.

RJ Publications
richjeanty@yahoo.com
www.rjpublications.com
Copyright © 2013 by Richard Jeanty
All Rights Reserved
ISBN 1939284023

Printed in the United States

April 2013

1 2 3 4 5 6 7 8 9 10

ACKNOWLEDGEMENTS

I would like to thank all the important people in my life who have supported me through my writing career and other endeavors. I stand strong because of you.

To my baby girl, Rishanna, you are growing up fast. I love you with all my heart. You continue to make my days brighter.

Special thanks go out to all the readers who continue to thirst for my writing. Without you, I'm nothing. I would like to give a big shout-out to the street vendors and booksellers around the country who are fighting to stay in the afloat, with the changing trends in the industry.

Special shout-outs go to all the New York book vendors and entrepreneurs. Special thanks to Hakim at Black and Nobel, Max in Brooklyn, Marcus at Nubian Bookstore in Atlanta, Horizon Books, my main man Chris B and and his son CJ, Pogo and Ali in the Bronx, and Henry in Harlem. I appreciate all of you.

A big shout-out goes out to my parents for bringing me to this world.

Special thanks go out to Annmarie Guzman for looking over my manuscript. You're a very special person.

Once again, I would like to dedicate this book to all the brothers and sisters who have forfeited their freedom justly and unjustly. Keep ya head up and keep the faith. Change is gonna come!

Introduction

I'm back at it again, writing about the most forbidden subject most of us enjoy almost everyday. None of us would be here if two people weren't having sex. This time, however, people might actually think that I'm a complete freak, because I take sexual enjoyment to another level.

When I decided to write a third part to this book, all kinds of different plots went through my mind. As a writer, I always believe my mind makes everything plausible, but that doesn't always equate to interesting. So, I took on the challenge and started writing something different. At first, the basic idea for the book was too easy a plot. One third into writing the book, I realized the plot or the path I was headed lacked entertainment. I decided to scrap the book and started over. Somehow, this book took on a life of its own the second time around. I know some people close to me will have many questions and their inquiring minds will try to attach as much of this book to me as possible. If only they knew the whole truth...

I'm gonna go out on a limb and say this is the most entertaining erotic novel I have ever written. I almost lost the zest for writing erotica until I revisited this series. Writing a character like Tina is fun, outrageous, liberating and sexy. I enjoyed every moment of this experience.

I trust that I can capture the readers' attention with this story from the very first page to the last. I always aim to entertain and educate with most of my works, but I hope this story opens the eyes and minds of many people who have not had the opportunity to experience anything like Tina's story. I know that I can't please everybody, but I hope that you can put into perspective that this is a fictional story about fictional characters, doing things that some of us may frown upon. For those of you who are open-minded enough to read this book without any prejudice, I say, "Get your freak on!"

Chapter 1

Darren and Tina were now known as Mr. and Mrs. Thomas to their new neighbors. A few months after they got married, Darren and Tina decided to sell their individual homes so they could purchase a home together. Though the housing market was slower than usual, Tina and Darren were able to sell their house just a few months after they got married. However, they couldn't maximize their profit, due to the housing market crash. Still, they both made enough of a profit to put a twenty-percent down payment on their new home in Woodmere, New York, a suburb of Long Island. The house was a steal, because it was a bank foreclosure. Somebody's misfortune became their fortune.

They walked away with a three-quarter million-dollar home for only half of a million. The four-bedroom, two and half baths and two-car garage home was large enough to accommodate Tina, Darren and the two children they were planning on having in the near future. The home is located on a quiet street off Peninsula Boulevard in a cul-de-sac. The location is perfect and the yard is just big enough for any family gatherings the two of them wanted to plan. The couple decided to move closer to the city because Darren had future plans and he wanted to be in an area that was easily accessible from the Long Island Expressway, and not too far from Manhattan. The couple enjoyed marital bliss from the time they left the altar. Darren and Tina couldn't keep their hands off each other. They finally did it, after all these years.

Tina's parents spared no expenses for their one and only daughter's wedding. It was a magical Winter in Wonderland theme with the extravagance of Hollywood. The couple looked magical and amazing. Darren's parents paid for the honeymoon in St. Maarten. Darren and Tina needed a vacation after exhausting themselves during the course of planning their wedding.

Darren and Tina hardly left the room after arriving at the exclusive Diamond Resorts Royal Palm Beach in St. Maarten. The secluded beach resort offered everything that Darren and Tina had on their wish list; tennis, golf, and the exuberance of Caribbean nightlife. The wide-eyed view of the inviting ocean offered calmness and a sexy mood for the couple. Darren almost wanted to rip Tina's clothes off as he stared into the distance of the never-ending ocean. The nicely blue and white decorated Cole Bay suite offered the kind of luxury created for a movie star. The plush mattress and thousand-thread-count linen felt great against Tina and Darren's skin as they plopped down to test the level of their comfort when they first entered the room. It was paradise on earth and they planned to maximize their time, enjoying the splendor of the country, as well as each other, during their honeymoon.

Since Tina and Darren were a little jet-lagged from the long flight, they decided they would rest on the first day of their honeymoon. However, they planned on exploring the beautiful island of St. Maarten as much as possible before leaving. A schedule of their activities was already created by Darren's parents, and it was up to them to either cancel or partake in some, or all of the activities. On the list were: catamaran day trip on the water, scuba diving, hiking, climbing the historic Mount Concordia and, of course, Da Party bus. There was an activity scheduled for each day they were going to spend on the island. Darren was excited as he showed Tina the brochure handed to every tourist arriving at the airport. There was an endless amount of activities listed in that brochure. However, he would be pleasantly surprised later that day when he found out that his parents had already taken care of everything for them. After setting their luggage down, the bed was a welcoming site to the two of them.

The first order of the day was a nap, so the couple could be well-rested before they went out on the town later. Darren's chiseled chest had become a cozy pillow for Tina whenever she wanted to rest. With his arm rested on Tina's back, it didn't take long for Darren to drift into a coma, while his wife fell into a dream state in the comfort of his arm. The sound of their breathing was almost harmonious in nature. Their hearts were beating as one as the two lovebirds lay in total calmness and enjoyed a moment of peace. They arrived in St. Marten around noon from their eight o'clock morning flight, but they wouldn't get up until six o'clock that evening when hunger started to set in.

The two of them woke up almost at the same time. "Damn, babe, your breath is tart," Tina told Darren playfully. "You just don't know, but I bet you can win a boxing fight with Tyson right now using your funky breath," Darren retorted. Tina did the breath test by holding her hand up to her mouth, "You're right. There's a lot funk going on in there." Darren smiled as he pulled his wife towards him for a kiss, funky breath and all. "I love you, woman, and it'll take more than funky breath to keep me away from you," he told her. Tina could only smile at her husband as she responded, "I love you too, stanky." The two of them got undressed, brushed their teeth and jumped in the shower together so they could hurry to the restaurant for dinner. However, the glistening water running down Tina's body in the shower put a damper on their haste plans for dinner. Darren couldn't help himself as he stared into Tina's brown eyes and realized there was a sudden blood flow rushing down to his crotch. Tina's reaction to his sudden erection also signified that a tingly sensation was taking place between her thighs as well. His right hand landed right on his dick, while her lips found his lips for a long kiss. The water dripped all over them. Darren slowly moved his hands down to Tina's round derriere, palming as much ass as his hands could grab, while he lost his tongue in her mouth. Their breathing was heavy as the two were entangled in a passionate kiss.

By now, Darren had learned his wife's body language, so he moved into the way of the water to shield Tina from getting her hair wet. Tina moved her lips slowly from his lips down to his chest past his six-pack abs and all the way down to the monster. She caught a handful of his manhood as she opened her mouth and wrapped her lips around his hardened dick. "Ooooh," he cooed at the smooth feeling of his wife's tongue around his dick. Darren reached for the wall for balance as Tina started to make him lose control in the shower. "Yeah, baby. Suck it," he instructed. Tina already knew that Darren was a sucker for her blowjobs. She took most of his dick inside her mouth, down her throat, while holding on to his buttocks. He humped her mouth slowly. She stood her ground and took his dick in like a trooper. Tina loved every inch of his dick. As Darren increased the speed of his movement, Tina backed off. She didn't want him to cum just yet. She stood up in front of him and leaned against the back wall, raising her leg on the side of the tub. Her full pinkness was exposed, and it was time for Darren to go to work. "Eat my pussy, baby," she said with a starving look on her face. As if she needed to ask? Darren moved away from the water and knelt down before Tina and commenced his pussy eating. His bald pate found comfort in her hands as Darren pulled the foreskin on her clit to expose her pinkness in his mouth. "Oh shit!" she screamed as the light stroke of his tongue on her clit got her more excited. Tina extended her pussy forward, while standing on her tippy toes and head rested on the back wall. Darren started to make her squirm with his tongue. "There it is, baby! Right there!" she yelled as a wave of ecstasy overtook her body. "I'm cummin', baby," she announced. Darren had taken her there many times before. He held her clit in his mouth and applied a little more pressure to intensify her climax. Tina came like it was clockwork.

She knew it wasn't over. Darren had held back for the big finish. Tina assumed the position of facing the wall, while resting her right leg up on the side of the tub to allow Darren easy penetrating access. After testing her pussy for lubrication with a finger or two, Darren deemed her pussy wet enough to absorb his dick. Though his fingers felt great inside of her pussy, Tina braced herself for the real penetration with his dick. Darren slowly inched his way into her pussy, making her feel every vein on his dick and every thrust of his stroke as he prepared to make her pussy hum. His strokes came from all directions as he enjoyed the wrath of Tina's tight pussy around his big dick. "Yes daddy! Fuck me. Fuck your pussy, baby." She cried tears of joy. "I love you, baby" he told her. "I love you, too, Darren. Fuck me, baby," Tina sulked in pleasure because Darren's dick felt so good to her.   Darren held on to her tiny waist as he did a slow-wind with his dick in Tina's pussy. "Yes!" he yelled. Tina knew what was coming. She especially liked Darren's violent strokes when he was cumming. She pushed her ass hard back towards him as he spanked her with both hands, trying to force his nut out. "Here it comes, baby," he told her, as he hit her with another long stroke coming all the way down from his knees. He poured all his love inside Tina, while holding her and shaking to the rhythm of their love sounds.

The two of them hurriedly finished their shower and got dressed in their casual summer wears. Darren wore grey linen shorts with a white short-sleeved linen shirt, and Tina wore a tan linen knot strap dress. While in the gastronomic capital of the Caribbean, Darren and Tina wanted to experience Caribbean dining at some of the finest restaurants on the island. A short cab ride to Phillipsburg landed them at Antoine's restaurant, for a taste of French Creole Cuisine. Chef Pierre Louis's finest dishes combined with some of the world's finest wine offered the most romantic dinner and a serene view of Great Bay.

The conversation flowed during dinner, and Tina and Darren couldn't be more in love. The body language between the two lovebirds was pure affection. Nothing could detract them from their love for each other. Finally, the couple found the bliss they had been working hard to establish. Darren and Tina spent seven days in St. Maarten, and they did everything they could possibly do to enjoy themselves, but more importantly, they made love to each other every chance they got.

Chapter 2

After Darren and Tina officially merged their families, the holidays were split between the two families. Tina and Darren spent Thanksgiving at her parents' house, while they spent Christmas with Darren's parents. However, one common question remained whenever Tina and Darren visited either side of their family, "When are the grandchildren coming?" Darren and Tina didn't succumb to the pressure from their family. They wanted to start a family on their own schedule. Though Tina was fast approaching thirty years old, she was in no rush to become a mother. Darren could never see himself as a dad, unless he was completely financially independent. He wanted to start a family when he was ready. He didn't want his work to take him away from his wife and children. His focus was to establish himself financially.

Darren had also been trying to decide on an ideal location for his new business where traffic and high visibility would help his business prosper. Darren already knew that location is an essential part of any business, so he wanted to make sure he didn't make the rookie mistake that most first-time business owners make, by having his business at the wrong location. He became his own scout in order to find the right location for his business. Every day after work, he went to different locations around town and sat in his car to monitor the foot traffic. Even on his days off, he would scout for locations without ever telling his wife about what he was doing. He didn't want to tell her anything until he was certain about his next move. Darren contemplated whether it was the right move to leave his now six-figure salary job to step out on his own. He wrestled with the idea for many months and wondered if Tina would stand behind him. Meanwhile, the idea of being newlywed was very attractive to them both and they wanted to live it up a little. He wanted to make his wife feel brand new until it never became old. Darren was the perfect husband, catering to his wife's every need. He would go to the end of the earth to make her happy, and she reciprocated.

Hanging out at the house on a rainy day watching movies all day was typical for them. *Love Jones, The Best Man*, and *The Brothers* are a few of their favorite movies, and they never grew tired of watching them together. They also spent time at the Roosevelt Field mall shopping whenever they needed to get out of the house. They did pretty much everything together and enjoyed being around each other as much as possible. It was hard for Darren to keep his scouting for a location for his business a secret much longer, but he managed to pull it off. Life was good, and it was about to get better. Darren especially enjoyed making love to his wife in the morning and one morning he gave her more than she ever bargained for. Tina relived that day in her head over and over again, and came each time she thought of it.

Chapter 3

"Damn, baby, you're tearing my pussy up! I don't know what's gotten into you this early in the morning, but I'm loving it," Tina told Darren, while one of her legs was up on the dresser as the rest of her body leaned forward to allow Darren's twelve-inch dick full entrance into her pussy. Since Tina and Darren got married, he made it his business to keep his wife sexually satisfied. Her sexual appetite never decreased and Darren figured he had to man up in order to please her. Sweat poured down his muscular frame as he stroked Tina hard, hoping she would climax at any moment, so he could rest for an hour or so before they went at it again. "Give it to me, baby," she moaned to encourage her husband's diligence to make her cum. Her sweet moans energized him. He slowly pulled his dick all the way out to the tip of his shaft, so she could feel the full throttle of his longness thrusting back in. The circumference of her opening wrapped tight around the head of his dick as he slowly stroked her pussy into submission. Tina's round booty had become Darren's natural aphrodisiac.

He would get hard at the site of her body stepping out of the shower, or whenever she came to bed wearing sexy lingerie to entice him. Tina was butt naked and exercising her pussy muscle to maximize the thrilling feeling of her husband's big cock inside her. Darren enjoyed the tightening of her pussy muscle even more as the pressure mounted and forced him to grab her ass tightly and poured all of his love inside her. There was hardly any room

- 15 -

between Darren's pubic area and Tina's ass, as his entire twelve-inch dick dug deep into her sugar wall. "I'm coming again, baby. Stay right there. Don't move," Tina ordered, as she grinded her way to another explosive nut. Darren simultaneously closed his eyes to allow his own explosion to come about, inside Tina's wet pussy. "I will never get tired of this pussy," he whispered, almost out of breath.

That was pretty much the routine for Tina and Darren whenever they spent too much time together in the house on the weekends. Rainy Saturdays basically consisted of hot sex, breakfast in bed, hot sex, take-out food, hot sex, rented movies, hot sex and then sleep. Darren had learned to reserve his energy for the rainy weekends to satisfy Tina's voracious sexual appetite. Darren also needed to conserve energy for work during the week. He needed to be focused in order to keep from making an accounting mistake on his clients' reports at work. Tina's pussy was always a distraction, though.

Burns and Young hired the best and brightest and Darren was definitely one of the best CPA's that firm had seen. During the week, Tina made use of all the toys she kept in the top drawer on the nightstand. Monday night was her rabbit night. That rabbit went through more batteries than a plumber's portable radio. Tina would spread her legs wide open on the bed, while laying on her back and her rabbit would be in her right hand, ready to eat her carrot.

One Monday night, Darren came home early to find his wife screaming at the top of her lungs, while the speed-control dial for the rabbit was on maximum. The pulsating vibration applied to her clit by the rabbit forced Tina's octaves to go up almost as high as an opera singer. If it were anybody else walking through that door, they would've panicked and looked for the biggest knife they could find before heading upstairs. Automatically, they would've thought someone was hurting Tina. However, Darren had gotten used to her screams. Tina could never contain her loud screams whenever she was experiencing what she called "an outer body experience" orgasm. Darren stood in the middle of the kitchen and smiled to himself before sneaking upstairs to watch Tina and the rabbit go to war with her clit. He had that devious look on his face as he stroked his penis in the buff, while standing at the door watching his wife with her eyes closed pleasing herself like the next nut meant the world to her. Darren had started taking off his clothes, while making his way up the stairs. By the time he reached the doorway, he only left his tie on, a hard dick in his hand, and the will to fuck his wife until she passed out.

Tina was pleasantly surprised when she opened her eyes to find a naked Darren, a wide grin and a hard twelve-inch dick ready to satisfy her even more. "Do you need any help with that nut?" Darren asked as he massaged the shaft of his dick with his hand. "I think my mouth might be more of service to that big dick of yours," Tina responded. Darren moved towards the bed as Tina lay on her stomach and reached for her favorite 12-inch bat. Darren's dick was rock hard and Tina's mouth was running like a faucet. She was especially happy to see him because Darren always worked extra late on Mondays, and he would come home tired to the point where he could only take a shower and go right to sleep.

The head of Darren's penis almost filled Tina's mouth as she wrapped her tongue around it before it disappeared into the warmth of her throat. It was soothing enough for Darren to close his eyes to allow the stress of his day to disappear from the forefront of his mind into the limited cluttered space he had in his brain. "Aaaaah," he whispered as Tina's magical tongue soothed the head of his hardened dick. With both hands on his hip, Darren stood there like a super hero, but he wasn't rescuing anybody, he was being rescued by his wife's tongue. Tina had conjured up enough tricks with her tongue to know exactly how to make her husband cum. She wrapped her tongue around his dick like she was tying a knot with a cherry stem in her mouth, and Darren knew he had to step back to keep from cumming prematurely. "Not yet, baby. I wanna enjoy your tongue. Don't make me cum yet," he begged. Tina smiled to herself because of the effect she knew she had on her husband. She sashayed her tongue down to his nuts and continued to massage them slowly. Darren reached for a handful of hair as his wife comforted his balls with her tongue.

Finally, Darren could wait no more. Tina's skin glistened under the dim light that cast a shadow against her beautiful round ass. Darren reached to caress it and lost control. He grabbed both cheeks with both hands as Tina took his long dick all the way down her throat. Darren had also discovered over time that Tina would lose control every time he massaged her anus. He used his middle finger to run circles around her anus, gently. Tina couldn't contain herself. "Fuck me! I want you to fuck me, baby," she begged. She spun around to bring her ass towards the edge of the bed so Darren could penetrate her from behind. He slowly entered, teasing the outer lips of her pussy with his gigantic dick. She shivered. She understood that his thrusts always made her lose control, so she grabbed a hand full of sheet for comfort as he dug deeper into her pussy. His dick was heavenly, totally incomparable to the feeling she received from the rabbit. This was the ultimate for her, penetration, no, Darren's penetration. He glided in and out of her slowly, while squeezing her ass cheeks just hard enough to excite her further. "Baby, your dick is so sweet. Give it to me," she lamented, because she had to use her rabbit before he walked in.

Darren never felt he was in competition with any of her sex toys, though. As a matter of fact, he started buying them for her. He wanted to keep her happy. The site of his beautiful wife kept his blood flowing and he wanted to please her. He augmented the speed of his strokes, because he knew and understood that she would soon command him to go faster. "You know how I like it, baby. Yes! Give it to me," she yelled. Darren obliged. He released his grip from her ass, so she could feel the sting of his smacks that would soon come. "Yeah, smack my ass, baby. Smack it like I'm on punishment, daddy" she said after the first sting. Darren knew her threshold for pain, so he added a little more force to the next few smacks on her ass, while he stroked her pussy hard, less the heinous brutality. There has never been a time when Tina didn't cum while Darren was fucking her from behind, and this time would be no different. Darren leaned his body forward and pushed himself deep inside Tina's pussy, allowing her to feel every inch of him, until she started rocking to the rhythm of his strokes and screaming, "I'm there, baby. I'm there. I'm fucking... cumming!" Darren was always proud of his work in the bedroom. It was now his turn to gather up his protein to make the dash to the finish line. He wrapped his hands around Tina's waist and brought his strokes from a squatting position up to a comfortable distance until he forced a nut out of his body into Tina's canal. He collapsed on top of her and she knew there would be no second round, at least, not on that Monday night.

Life had been pretty easy since Darren and Tina got married. They also decided to delay having children because they wanted to spend more time with each other before bringing kids into the world. In addition, Darren wanted to travel the world with his lovely wife. Though he worked long hours and spent way too much time at work, Darren had accumulated a significant amount of vacation time at work. His boss was always forcing him to go on vacation, but he refused. The last vacation he took with Tina was his honeymoon trip to St. Maarten, and prior to that, they had gone to Barbados. It was those memories that brought a smile to his face every time he thought about traveling to a foreign country with his wife. However, Darren had a goal and he wasn't ready to reveal it to his wife yet. He worked so hard and saved his money, because owning his own accounting firm was something he had been dreaming about since he passed his CPA exam. It was while he was in bed with Tina one night he decided to let her in on his plans to leave his job the upcoming year. Tina was in a great mood because Darren had forced a multitude of orgasms out of her body with his tongue and his even more pleasing dick. It was time for him to let the cat out the bag. He had earned stock options, a 401K plan and had earned enough vacation time that equaled three months of his salary, should he ever decide to cash it in.

Darren thought long and hard about his decision, but he knew he had to go with his heart. The short long-weekend trips to Miami, Atlantic City, the Poconos and Las Vegas had become routine in Darren and Tina's life, but it was time to travel beyond the United States. He knew his wife was looking forward to one of those long vacations around Europe or a Safari in Africa, but the time wasn't right yet. Darren needed to maintain his focus and he decided that he would wait a little while longer before taking his wife to Europe or Africa on her dream vacation.

After Darren let Tina in on his plan to start his own firm, Tina played the role of supporting wife and decided not to press the issue with her husband. Darren's happiness was the ultimate to her and she didn't feel complete unless her husband was happy in every aspect of his life. Besides, she also understood that Darren was a visionary and he was planning for their future. She was elated that he was gutsy enough to go out and make his dream a reality.

Chapter 4

After Darren finally made the hard decision to leave his job to start his own accounting firm, Tina stood firmly behind her husband and offered all the support he needed. Office space was essential to his business, so Darren decided to open his office in Five Towns, an area in New York where five different towns are connected. The traffic in the area was perfect and Darren wouldn't have to worry so much about building his clientele, he could focus on growing his business. In addition, Darren had personal clients whose taxes he had been doing for years while he was working for corporate America, and those clients planned on following him to his private practice. Things were looking up as he devised his plan for a solid, long-lasting business. First, Darren needed to rent office space and that task would prove to be daunting, simply because of Darren's complexion.

The most perfect and affordable space available to him was owned by an older white man who wasn't too fond of the African race. Even though the sign on the property clearly stated "Space Available for Rent," Darren got a different response when he met with the owner face to face. The old racist guy had no idea that Darren was black during their conversation over the phone. Darren had faxed all the necessary documents required for the rental and had proven to the man that he had enough money in his bank account to sustain the rent for the length of the year's lease, and his credit was impeccable. The only thing left to do was to sign the lease. The fact that Darren's credit score was above 800 was the first thing that jumped out to the owner of the building. It was very impressive, the old man thought. However, when the old man finally met Darren in person, his opinion of the perfect tenant, based on Darren's credit and credentials, changed. He found every excuse he could use to keep the property from Darren. They had agreed on a one-year lease, with the exclusive right for Darren to sign a five-year lease at the end of the year, but the man stated he wanted a ten-year lease and Darren had to prove that he had at least two years' worth of rental income held in an escrow account in order to get the property. He already knew that was impossible. The old man reneged and it was obvious why he didn't want to rent to Darren. With very little time to waste, Darren moved on with his search, but not before he hired a lawyer and filed a multi-million dollar suit against the racist landlord for not renting to him. He knew the case would be caught up in litigation for a while, but he was willing to wait just to teach that man a lesson and obtain justice.

Darren eventually was able to get a much better space from a Jewish man who owned a newly built strip mall. The rent was also a third less than he anticipated paying monthly, based on his budget. The Jewish man was impressed with Darren's background and knew that success would be a matter of time. Darren was happy to secure a location. The work was just beginning. Like most entrepreneurs, Darren spent more time working to establish his business than he did while he was working for a corporation. He understood the first year was crucial to his success, because most small businesses fail during the first year. Darren relied heavily on word of mouth and referrals and Tina made it her business to spread the word as much as possible to her friends and associates. She even convinced her father to fire his accountant of twenty years, so that Darren could have the account. It wasn't really that hard of a decision, because her father cared more about her well-being and he wanted to help the young couple in any possible way he could. The fact that her father was also fond of Darren and thought he was a stand-up guy, also helped. Tina didn't have to convince her brother, Will, who decided to have Darren do his taxes as well. The future seemed bright and things were looking up.

One of the things Tina decided to do in order to help Darren with his new business was attending these networking mixers. Since Darren was busy at work, she had to find something to occupy her time after work. She was pretty much running her father's company, and business had doubled in the past year. Still, Tina never went out of her way to make Darren feel less than a man when she offered financial assistance for his business, in case he needed it. She also knew that Darren wanted to build his business his way, without the financial contribution of her family. Darren also knew that if he did a great job with Will's taxes, his celebrity client list would shoot through the roof. All of Will's NFL buddies would be referred to him and those types of clients alone would sustain his business. Darren set out to be a self-made man.

Tina gave Darren his space and time so he could focus on growing his business. Sex had become routine for a little while, because Darren was often tired and thinking about innovative ways to grow his business. However, the two of them kept the communication lines open. There were times when a quickie on the staircase was satisfying enough for Tina. The excitement of Darren just pinning her on the stairway in the house before he even penetrated her was enough to bring her orgasm to the forefront. By the time his penis made contact with her pussy, Tina would often cum over and over. Those climactic episodes were more psychological than physiological. Still, Tina didn't complain. Darren even became a little creative in order to keep his wife satisfied. More often than not, he would use his lunch hour to surprise Tina at the office with roses and a bottle of champagne before pinning her on the desk for a quickie on his way out the door. The idea alone was exhilarating enough to hold Tina's interest.

Darren also learned firsthand that establishing a new business was no easy task. Taking on so many clients meant more overhead and more people needed to be hired. The bottom line, Darren had to sacrifice making less money in order to serve his clients properly. No one can run a business successfully without any hired help. Darren learned that very quickly. However, it would take a lot of trust to allow an employee full access to his clients' files. An assistant was needed as soon as possible and Darren called on his wife to help hire one. An ad was placed in the local newspaper, online, and posted on his business' Facebook page. The responses were insurmountable, because of the bad economy. Many women applied, but few were qualified for the position. The few who were unqualified wore the shortest and tightest skirts and blouses to the interview, in order to increase their chances of being hired. While Tina may have been the initial interviewer, Darren was clearly the person to make the final decision. Darren and Tina saw more tits and asses hanging out of clothing during the interview period than they had seen in their lifetime. The two of them joked about the lack of shame and pride shown by some of the women who came dressed scantily clad to the interview. There was this one girl who impressed Tina and Darren very much.

This beautiful 5ft 7-inch tall, dark-colored skin sister had the whitest teeth, highest cheekbones, sexy full lips, nice round African nose with small nostrils, almond eyes, shoulder-length hair, and the sexiest body a woman that size could carry. She was a solid size eight with a body more curvaceous than a video vixen. Her beauty was made for magazine covers. She was what most men might refer to as a "brick house." Her stomach was flat and her round butt looked as firm as a Sealy mattress. Most of the time, women with nice bottoms usually lack more than a little bit up top, but this woman broke the mold. She was not typical in any way. Her perfect 36C cups accented the complete package from top to bottom. She had been a secretary with another small business that went under during the economic slide. She seemed efficient, knowledgeable and talented enough for the position during her interview. However, she was also extremely reserved and shy. Darren and Tina both agreed she was the best candidate for the position, but Darren could sense apprehension and reservation from his wife about the decision. "Babe, I know you're not gonna start tripping because this woman is attractive. She's got nothing on my wife. Besides, I need an attractive woman in the office in order to keep my customers coming back, especially when I start getting the accounts from the athletes," he tried to reason with Tina. She reluctantly agreed to hire the girl, whom she felt was the most qualified among all the candidates, anyway.

Abigail Steele was to be the new hire and was slated to start working the upcoming Monday. Abigail wore one of her most conservative attires to the interview, a grey pinstripe pantsuit, white shirt, medium heels, wire rimmed glasses, her hair pinned up and a a bag over her shoulders. She looked the part and demonstrated the ability to conquer the job. Darren was excited about his new hire and he was looking forward to having her in the office the following week to help alleviate some of his duties. Finally, he could just concentrate on what he knew best, preparing taxes. The meeting ended with a handshake and a promise of a follow-up phone call. Darren didn't want to seem desperate; he didn't offer Abigail the job on the spot. He needed to check out the three references she listed on her application to make sure her résumé was real. Tina volunteered to do the reference check. Since Tina had been running her father's company for a few years now, she knew the pertinent questions she needed to ask in order to field the right answers.

Tina immediately went to work after leaving Darren's office. She found it kind of odd that two of Abigail's references had cell phones, as her calls went straight to voicemail. Still, she tried to keep an open mind because in this new age of technology, most people run their business with cell phones. She was able to get in touch with the person Abigail last worked for, and the man had nothing but praise for Abigail's discipline, work habit and her tenacity for details. It was a very impressive reference. The man stated that he would have kept Abigail working indefinitely if his company didn't file for bankruptcy. Abigail had never mentioned that the company she worked for filed for Chapter 11. She simply stated they went out of business. Tina found it kind of odd, but she relegated it to an oversight.

She would eventually receive calls from the other two references, for which she left messages, but those references seemed to be more personal. Against her better judgment, she decided that the first guy was polished enough and she was worth taking a chance. She called Darren to let him know how she felt about the possible hire, while also suggesting to go through a few more applicants applying for the job. "Tina, you know the one thing I don't have right now is time. I'm already swamped, and if you feel this girl can do the job, let's hire her," he told her. "I just want you to be safe than sorry, Darren. I'm not saying this girl is not qualified to do the job, but I'm a bit suspicious of her references. That's all," she told him. Darren had to think about his wife's statement before responding. He looked around in his office and saw the pile of files sitting on his desk and thought about the promise he made to his clients that their taxes would be completed on time. "Babe, I know you have my best interest at heart, but I'm also looking at a ton of possible clients' folders sitting on my desk right now that I may lose if I don't complete these taxes by next week. I say, let's hire her and if any problem arises, we can always fire her," he assured her. "Ok, just remember it was your decision, not mine," she warned. "I understand," he said to confirm Abigail for the position.

After getting off the phone with Darren, Tina placed a call to Abigail to offer her the position. Abigail was ecstatic and couldn't wait to start the job. She thanked Tina multiple times for hiring her. Tina felt a little better about the hire because she could hear Abigail choking on her tears, like a door had been opened for her. She was given her dignity back, as she had been unemployed for close to a year. Tina felt good that she played a role in helping a woman get her self-esteem back. She got off the phone feeling confident she had done a good deed. Her reservations about Abigail started to wane almost instantly.

Chapter 5

Darren felt like the weight of the world had been lifted off his shoulders after he received the phone call from Tina, telling him that Abigail had accepted his offer for the position at a salary of thirty eight thousand dollars annually. She told Darren that she made it clear to Abigail it was a salaried position and sometimes she would have to work a little late. Darren was happy that Tina actually paid attention to the fact that he sometimes has to work late and a little help would go a long way. Abigail agreed that staying late occasionally was not a problem. However, the salary offered didn't really reflect all the work that they intended for her to do. Nonetheless, she needed a job and the economy wasn't about to get better any time soon. It was a steal for Darren.

Since it was a Friday night, Darren and Tina decided to go out to dinner to celebrate. Easing Darren's work schedule meant more sex for Tina and more time with her husband. She was happy about that. Darren saw it as an opportunity to enjoy the little moments with his wife as well. The two of them were still on their newlywed high and it was cute that they wanted to relish the moment. They arrived in separate cars at the restaurant where they'd planned to meet. Reservations were set for 7 PM, but Darren was running about five minutes late. He had to make a few phone calls before leaving the office, and he received a phone call from Abigail, asking about how she would be paid and whether it was weekly, bi-weekly or a monthly payroll system. Darren thought nothing of it, but he put it on the back of his mind. She hadn't started working yet, but she wanted to know the pay schedule? That was normal, he thought. Most employees want to know their pay schedule from their employer, including Darren who asked the very same question when he was hired at his last job. He told her that would be part of her orientation when she reported to work on Monday.

Darren finally made it to the restaurant around ten minutes past seven o'clock. He asked the maitre d if his wife had shown up, but the Maitre D pointed to a woman sitting at the table who didn't look familiar at all to Darren. She was the only woman in the restaurant wearing shades and her long black hair was totally opposite of Tina's medium length hairstyle. Darren was about to say something to the Maitre D when the woman noticed him and motioned for him to come over with her finger. He was a little reluctant to go over at first, but he didn't want to be rude. He looked around to make sure his wife wasn't anywhere in the vicinity, before he walked over to find out what the woman wanted. "You seem like you're lost, are you looking for anybody in particular?" the woman asked in her most seductive voice. "Well, I'm actually looking for my wife. We have a date here tonight, but I don't think she's arrived yet," Darren told her. "Why do you think she's late?" the woman asked. "I don't know, but that's not like her. I'm usually the late one," Darren told the woman as he impatiently looked back towards the entrance to see if he could spot his wife. "I'm sorry, I have to go. I need to find out why my wife is not here," Darren told the woman who was wearing an overcoat. She kept her face in the menu, so Darren was only able to see part of her profile. As Darren turned to leave, the voice said, "I'm Trina, the alter ego of Tina. Sit down, baby." Darren was shocked his wife was so unrecognizable. He shook his head in amazement as Tina continued to disguise her voice as a sexy kitten.

Finally, Darren pulled his chair and took a seat. "You know? You are one crazy woman. Where'd you get that wig you're wearing?" he asked. "I don't know what you're talking about. My name is Trina and I've always looked like this. And guess what?" she asked. "There's more... what?" Darren asked with curiosity. "I'm not wearing anything under this coat, we better hurry with dinner, so your dessert can still be fresh when we get home," Tina teased. Darren could only shake his head at the situation. Darren quickly motioned for the waiter to bring two menus. They both decided to skip the appetizers and went straight for the main course. Seafood is a known aphrodisiac and Darren couldn't pass up the opportunity to increase his libido. He ordered especially-made oysters in a pasta sauce. Tina didn't need any help with her libido. Her sex drive was always on high. She ordered a lobster dish with mashed potato. Darren also ordered a couple of glasses of wine to help him ease his mind. Tina chose cabernet. The two barely spoke over dinner as their focus remained on the task ahead at home. Meanwhile, Tina spread her legs open under table before reaching for Darren's hands so he could feel her moistened pussy. He took his finger to his mouth and confirmed that she never tasted better. Needless to say, dinner was brief.

Darren wasted no time settling his tab. He had Tina on his mind and he couldn't wait to get home to thrill her. Since they drove separate cars to the restaurant, Darren decided to make a bet with Tina before they left. "If I make it home before you, I want you to suck me until your jaws hurt tonight," Darren teasingly told Tina. She knew it was a task because Darren didn't cum easily through oral. "If I make it home before you, I want you to tie me up to the bed and fuck me until my pussy can't take it anymore," Tina proposed. Now Darren knew he had better beat Tina to the house, because her sexual appetite was huge and it could be hours before Tina was completely satisfied. They agreed on the bet with a kiss before they both dashed off to their cars.

Once Darren got in his car, he picked up his phone and dialed his wife. The automated Bluetooth in Darren's car captured Tina's voice, "Hi baby," she answered in her car through her own automated Bluetooth. "I hope you're exercising those lips, because you're gonna be sucking this dick for a long time tonight," Darren teased. "I guess you must be flooring it, because I was thinking you should've ordered a Red Bull, since you're gonna need all your energy to fuck me tonight," Tina retorted. "We'll see about that. This hard dick has your name written all over it, and I can't wait to stand in front of the bed with my hands on my hip like Superman while you suck the skin off it with those pretty lips of yours," Darren teased again. "I'm gonna suck your big, hard dick alright, but my throbbing pussy is telling me that your big dick is gonna make it purr all night. How about that, baby? Are you ready to make my pussy purr?" Tina teased. "Where you at? Cause my dick is as hard as steel and I'm just waiting for you to wrap your tongue around it. I might consider making your pussy purr after I win the bet." Darren started to bend a little. "Guess what? I might consider sucking that delicious dick of yours a little longer than usual when I beat you home tonight, but my pussy is soaked and wet and waiting for your slow penetration. I will see you when I get home. Bye." Tina hung up so she could focus on the road.

Darren already knew there was no way he was just gonna stand there and have Tina please him without returning the favor. He was more anxious to get to her goods than ever before. The idea of Tina being bold enough to leave the house wearing a raincoat and nothing more was exciting to Darren. He couldn't wait to beat her home and he knew just the right short cut. Darren dashed in and out of traffic like a mad man with his hard dick ready to explode. He beat Tina home just in the nick of time. By the time she opened the door to the kitchen, Darren was leaning against the door frame butt naked with his hands on his waist, a smile on his face, a rose clinched between his teeth, hard dick filled with blood and a smile across his face. "Are you ready to serve your master?" he asked, while smiling. She smiled back at him as he handed her the single red rose. "You think this rose is gonna make you look good? You're not earning any brownie points from me," she said with a devilish smile. "Is that right? Maybe I need to be your bad boy tonight?" he suggested. "So what you're gonna do to me, bad boy?" she asked in her most seductive voice. "For starters, bring your ass over here and let me see what you got under that coat," Darren said. Tina started strutting towards him and spun around so he could get a 360 degree view as she opened her coat. "You wear that birthday suit well," he said as he stared at Tina's sexy naked body, while she stood in the middle of the living room in 5-inch heels. Darren started stroking his dick slowly as Tina stared at him. His glistened, lubricated body made her mouth run like a river. "I think you need to come over here and help me with this as much as you can," he said as he pulled on his 12-inch dick. "At your service, daddy," Tina replied as she assumed the position before his majesty.

A bet was a bet and Darren won. Tina got into a squatting position like a stripper around a stripping pole with a look of hunger in her eyes, while she stared up at Darren with his thick, long dick in her hand. Darren started smirking a little as he took in the habitual dick massage from his wife. Darren was staring right into Tina's eyes as she voraciously slid her tongue around his dick, while looking up at him. She wanted him to submit to her special skills. She watched him until he could no longer stand the sensation of her tongue on his dick, and had to forcibly close his eyes. The big sigh released by Darren confirmed that Tina's skills hadn't diminished and her husband very much still enjoyed her passionate tongue. He no longer leaned against the wall. He stood straight with his hand landing on the back of Tina's head, grabbing her hair and helping to maneuver her head movement back and forth. Tina took the opportunity to seduce her husband further by inserting her middle finger in her pussy. Her movements were motioned by her own moans of pleasure. Tina's kitten-like moans drove Darren wild. He soon found himself trying to hump her mouth. She slid his dick in and out of her mouth, while she massaged the tip with her fingers. Darren couldn't stand it and it was something new that Tina had picked up from watching a porno flick. She kept his dick lubricated by spitting in her hand and rubbing it up and down as she caressed the shaft with her tongue. Landing time was near and even faster than usual. Darren spread his arm around the door frame holding on, while leaning back to let out a loud roar as Tina made him cum in a more intense way than ever before. She sucked every drop of protein out of his dick, until he begged for her to stop. "You didn't know I had a surprise for you, huh?" Tina said, while winking at him. He was silent. He knew he had better bring something new when he started to eat her pussy, while she sat on the couch.

The full view of Tina's pussy before Darren as she held her legs up wide open in front of him was celestial. Her 5-inch heels made her look even sexier as she cocked her head back waiting for him to devour her. He stuck a finger in and took it to his mouth to get a taste of her sweet nectar. "Mmm... my favorite flavor, your pussy tastes like water... fresh and clean," he said as he bent down to take a whiff. Darren buried his nose deep inside Tina's pussy to inhale her clean scent. He grabbed her by the ass cheeks and lifted her a little bit off the couch. Tina didn't know what hit her when Darren stuck his tongue in her ass. "Oh shit!" she exclaimed as the touch of his tongue around the rim of her anus caused a tingling sensation she had never felt before. Around and around he went with his tongue and Tina could barely stand it. She shook and grabbed his head for comfort.

He continued to eat her ass because she didn't know what to do with herself. Then he went from her ass to her pussy making a straight line from one erogenous zone to another. The combination of ass and pussy licking forced Tina to breathe heavily, as if her normal breathing couldn't bear the sensitivity of Darren's tongue around her anus. "What the fuck? You never ate my ass like that before. You're killing me with this shit. I fucking love you!" she confessed once more. Darren knew he was up to something good whenever Tina professed her love for him in a profane way. He lifted her off the couch upside down and wrapped her legs around his neck with her pussy landing right on his face. Tina hung suspended with her face swinging around Darren's stiff dick. She couldn't help herself as she reached and took it in her mouth, forcefully. Darren could sense her voracity. He stuck his thumb halfway in her ass, while he tongue-fucked her.   Tina's body started shaking as Darren double-penetrated her with his tongue and thumb. She was about to explode. She never relented on his dick as she tightened her legs around his neck to allow her cream fillings to exit her body. Darren held on tight to her ass as she started the gyration of her pussy all over his mouth as she came.

Tina's hair was all over her face after Darren placed her back down on the couch. The wig had fallen off and her hair looked wild. She was almost out of breath, because she couldn't believe that Darren had made her cum in a manner that was foreign to her. It was on from then on. After catching her breath, Tina leaned forward towards the back of the couch and knelt on the seating part of the cushion as her ass was raised up. The wide view of Tina's sexy ass was intrusive and Darren couldn't help himself. He rubbed his finger on his tongue a couple of times before parting Tina's pussy, while rubbing her clit to ensure her pussy was moist enough. Confident that she was well-lubricated, he proceeded to slide into her inch by inch. Darren took a hold of her ass cheeks as he slowly entered her legion of pleasure. Her pussy was warm and elastic around his dick as he slowly stroked her. The visual before him was enough to force an early ejaculation out of him, but Darren focused his mind elsewhere. He wanted to enjoy the session with his wife. Meanwhile, Tina couldn't help talking to her husband, telling him how good his dick felt. "Fuck your pussy, baby. Your dick is so sweet," she said through clinched teeth. Smack! Smack! Tina felt the sensation of Darren's hands across her butt cheek and that sent her into a groove. She started moving her ass like she was "Twerking" to a reggae song and then slowed it down with a Reggae wind. "I love this pussy, babe," Darren told his wife. "I know, baby. This pussy loves you, too," she confirmed. Though Darren wanted to make the session last a little longer, he couldn't help cumming when Tina started playing with her clit, while moving her ass up and down on his dick. "I'm cumming, baby. Ooooh!" he screamed as his thick semen drenched Tina's pussy.

Darren and Tina went upstairs, took a shower and fell asleep in each other's arms while watching ESPN. Needless to say, they both slept like babies through the night. However, that episode would be repeated over and over throughout the weekend.

Chapter 6

Darren reported to his office bright and early on Monday morning. The business hours posted on the front of his office stated 9 AM to 6PM, but it was very rare that Darren showed up past 8:30 AM. He was an early riser and a motivator. Procrastination is not a word found in Darren's vocabulary. He didn't believe in it. Darren was pleasantly surprised when Abigail showed up at 8:30AM instead of the 9:00AM scheduled time. She earned brownie points with him right away. As an Administrative Assistant, Abigail's general job description was as follows: Report to Darren and provide administrative support to him; assuming bookkeeping, reservations and reception. These duties included but were not limited to: database system maintenance and training, office supply purchasing, typing, filing, reception and telephone duties. Since Abigail received her Bachelor's Degree in Business Administration, Darren assumed she had the capacity and the intelligence to perform those duties. However, Darren still wanted confirmation that Abigail was indeed qualified for the position. The first assignment he gave her when she came in was a letter that he had written to a company trying to solicit business from them. He purposely misspelled a few words in the letter to see if Abigail would notice and call it to his attention. She passed with flying colors and the letter was on his desk within minutes. "That was fast," he said to her when she approached him with the letter in her hand. "I also found a few mistakes that you made, I hope you don't mind that I corrected them," she told him in a shy way.

Darren hadn't really taken inventory of Abigail's outfit and her overall look when he first saw her that morning. He was preoccupied with the file of a client that was more pertinent at the time, but he soon noticed that the woman he had hired was a total bombshell on the morning she showed up for work. Abigail Steele was dressed in the sexiest outfit she could find in her closet that morning. If Tina laid eyes on her, she would've sent her home right away. It didn't seem like she showed up to work, but to steal Tina's husband. Her short black tightly fitted mini skirt barely rested on her thighs and her fitted white button-down collared shirt accentuated her bosoms to the point where Darren had to say something to her. While taking inventory of her stroll into his office, Darren couldn't help but stare at her long legs sitting on four-inch stiletto heels, making her look like she was looking for upward mobility in the corporate world. Her look was reminiscent of what Darren was accustomed to seeing in corporate America. Women who dressed like that were looking to move up in the company. "While I think your outfit looks great on you, I don't think it's appropriate for you to wear a skirt that short to the office again. Also, I would loosen the shirt and button it up a little bit," Darren told her. Abigail smiled and said, "I'm sorry. I wasn't sure what the dress code required. At my last job, I could wear anything I wanted as long as it looked professional." Darren didn't really know what to say, but the fact that he could see Abigail's red thong when she bent over to file a folder in the cabinet was evidence enough that her skirt was too short. "My wife is a very observant woman and she may drop by here sometimes and I don't want her to say the wrong thing to you. I just think it might be better if you toned it down a little," Darren said to her. "Won't happen again," she said, while holding in her tempted grin.

Though Darren used caution to make sure things didn't get out of hand with Abigail on the very first day, he couldn't help himself for the rest of the day. He took quick glances at her ass and her thighs whenever she wasn't looking his way. Abigail's sexy toned legs were smooth and silky and her juicy butt almost caused Darren to get an uncontrollable erection. He knew then that it was going to be hard to work with Abigail. It would take all of his self-control to keep from making advances towards her, something he honestly didn't want to do. The best solution was to keep his door closed for the rest of the day and avoid contact with Abigail as much as possible.

After completing her first assignment of alphabetically filing the clients' files in the cabinet, Abigail knocked on Darren's door to get a new assignment from him. "I'm done filing all of the files you gave me, is there something else that you'd like me to do?" she asked while leaning down over his desk exposing a little too much cleavage for Darren to bear. Her perky breasts were inviting, her lips were lusciously covered with burgundy lipstick and for the first time, Darren noticed that her eyes had a light brown hue. Abigail left the eyeglasses at home and wore her hair down past her shoulders. "Are you wearing contacts?" Darren asked. Abigail smiled before answering, "Yes. Why do you ask?" Darren was just curious if she was wearing colored contacts because he didn't really pay much attention to her eyes when he initially saw her at the interview. "Well, that color looks good on you," he said nonchalantly. "Why do you mean?"She asked confusingly. "Those colored contacts don't always look good on black women, but they go well with your complexion," Darren told her. "Oh, ok. These are not colored contacts. They are my eyes. I got them from my mama," she said as she pointed to her light brown eyes. "I'm sorry. I didn't mean to offend you. I just remember that you were wearing glasses when you came to the interview and I can't recall what your eyes looked like. My apologies," Darren said sentimentally. "No offense taken. Ever since I was a little girl, people have always assumed that I'm wearing colored contacts because my eyes are light. I don't know where these eyes originated from, but my grandmother's eyes are the exact same color, so they must've come from her side of the family," she told Darren. "Well, you have beautiful eyes then," Darren said trying to smooth things over with her.

The rest of day went by without a hitch and Abigail seemed like she was a fast learner and a reliable employee thus far. Darren couldn't believe how shapely Abigail was and how her dark chocolate complexion radiated every time he looked at her. That could possibly create problems for him, he thought. Then again, it wouldn't be fair to fire her because she was an attractive woman. He suggested she took a lunch break around noon, and that gave him time to cool off and figure out a way to be around this gorgeous woman. While Abigail was at lunch, he was thinking about the best way to interact with her without crossing the line. He loved his wife and wanted to remain faithful to her, but a beautiful woman has been known to be a weakness for most men. Abigail was also a little flirtatious, which Darren tried to dismiss. Darren knew he couldn't mention a word about Abigail's attire to his wife when he got home, or the way she looked. He was happy when five o'clock came around. He told Abigail she could leave and he stayed in the office for an extra hour doing a little bit of work, but was more trying to collect himself before he went home. He closed the office around six o'clock in the evening and went home.

Chapter 7

Darren got home that evening and tried his best to act as normal as possible around his wife. It was as if he had done something wrong and was feeling guilty about it. "So, how was Abigail's first day at the office?" Tina asked, while sitting on the couch cuddling with her husband watching television. Though Tina didn't cook every day, she occasionally came home early to treat her husband to a nice dinner. She enjoyed sitting at the table with her husband, while they have dinner together, sometimes. This particular evening, Darren was more quiet than usual. Tina followed his lead and didn't say much while they were at the table eating dinner. He thanked her after he was done, went and took a shower before settling down on the couch with his wife. All kinds of thoughts ran through Darren's minds as he tried to figure out the best answer to Tina's questions.

"Today was an interesting day," he said. Tina's curiosity grew. "What do you mean by interesting?" she asked. "Oh, nothing," Darren shook his head to help wane her interest. "Come on, you can't say it was interesting without giving me some details," Tina said encouragingly. "Well, I was shocked that Abigail came in so early this morning. She wasn't supposed to start work until 9 AM, but she showed up a half hour early. Also, she seems to absorb directions very easily. I think she'll be alright," he said trying to dismiss Tina's quest for more truth. "Well, I had a feeling about her. I think she'll work out, but be careful because you can never let your guard down with an attractive woman," she advised. "Believe me, I'm gonna be as careful as I can, working with this woman in my office," Darren said as his tongue slipped and took the conversation somewhere Tina never expected. "What do you mean, you're gonna be as careful as you can, working with her in your office? Is there something you're not telling me?" she asked with her curiosity piqued. Darren tried to divert his attention elsewhere to avoid an argument with his wife, "Let's just watch your favorite show and enjoy the evening," he suggested by switching the channel to one of Tina's girly shows, Basketball Wives.

Darren was saved by the asinine antics of two basketball groupies making an ass out of themselves on television. Tina's focus was now on the cat fight between the two female cast members who called themselves basketball wives, but neither was married to a basketball player. That show was Tina's guilty pleasure. She loved the "rachetness" going on with these silly women on television, trying to capitalize on the fact that a ball player may have bedded them. Basically, they were former groupies turned opportunists, looking for a payday. It was black entertainment at its worst, setting the Civil Rights movement fifty years back. Tina loved it and it saved Darren that night. The conversation didn't come up again because Darren knew just what to do to keep his wife's mind free and clear of his office. After the show, Darren and Tina went to their room and he used his tongue in ways that would make a mother forget her child at the mall. Tina had so many orgasms, the only thing she could do after

Darren was done was go to sleep. Darren chuckled to himself at the sound of his wife's light snores. He had won the fight that night, but he knew the battle wasn't over. Tina would possibly visit that conversation again, and he had better prepared himself for it.

Darren hardly got any sleep that night. He tossed and turned all night long. He even had a dream that night, and in his dream, he was doing things that he wasn't supposed to be doing…"Bend over the desk," Darren commanded Abigail as he pulled up her skirt and let himself into her wet pussy. "Yeah, that's how you want it? Tell me, you like this dick!" Darren screamed as he smashed Abigail's pussy from the back. Darren's dick was rock hard as he grabbed his wife in a dream state trying to release his tension in his sleep. Tina obliged him by pushing her ass towards him in a spooning comfortable way. Darren's dick was deep inside her pussy as he fucked her hard in his sleep. Meanwhile, in Darren's dream, Abigail's pussy couldn't be any tighter. "Oh yeah, that pussy's tight just like daddy likes it. Tina had never been fucked by Darren, while he was having a wet dream; this was a first for her. Darren ferociously stroked her pussy and Tina stood her ground to take every inch of his dick. "Flip over. Get on your back," Darren ordered as Abigail got on the desk to get on her back. Her purplish pink pussy was wide open as Darren began his invasion. He pulled her towards him, while her legs rested on his arms. He wanted his full length inside of her. "Yes daddy!" she screamed, encouraging Darren to fuck her harder. He stroked her pussy hard as he sucked on her toes. "Gimme that dick, Daddy!" she yelled. Anticipating his nut nearing,

Darren screamed, "I'm cumming! Take it in your mouth!" Tina shifted position and placed her mouth on Darren's dick. Like most men who have wet dreams, Darren was shocked when he opened his eyes to find Tina's mouth wrapped around his dick. "You were great, baby," Tina told him. Only if she knew he was fucking Abigail in his dream.

Chapter 8

Almost a year had gone by, and everything was going well in the office between Darren and Abigail. She had toned down her sexy way of dressing. Darren no longer walked around trying to keep his dick from getting hard because of the way she dressed. Abigail's business suits covered most of her assets, but they were tastefully sexy. Darren had come to appreciate her hard work and dedication. The two of them were growing comfortable around each other. Darren started to trust Abigail a little more and he also started to relinquish more of his responsibilities to her. Abigail was fond of the newfound trust bestowed upon her by Darren and she appreciated him for it. There were times when the two of them had lunch together at the office, whenever Darren decided to treat her to Chinese food. Business also started to pick up and Darren knew that he had to start delegating even more work to Abigail.

The professional relationship between Abigail and Darren grew customarily. He learned to trust her and he believed in her instincts. Abigail now became responsible for not only receptionist and administrative duties, but also to solicit clients and refer them for appropriate services; she cooperated in the maintenance and modification data collection system for Darren's agency; she oversaw database management for quality assurance; she maintained accurate daily accounting of fees, and other revenues for the business; she assisted with completion of necessary statistical reports, whenever possible; she compiled statistical information for Darren as needed; she developed and maintained agency inventory system; she filtered incoming calls and prepared outgoing mail, including bulk mail; she maintained front desk area, keeping it clean and free from clutter; typed and word processed documents as needed; she ordered office supplies and monitored inventory; she updated and maintained mailing lists; she produced mailing labels and reports as requested; she maintained appropriate interpersonal relationships with clients and other consumers; and she facilitated special event registration and execution. Abigail had total access to Darren's business. With that knowledge, she also gained access to the bank statements for the business and knew exactly the amount of money Darren was bringing in every month. It was time for her to demand a raise, after a year into her position, which Darren felt was fair. Abigail wanted a bigger piece of the pie.

Abigail had proven to Darren she was very proficient in all of the areas necessary and the duties he had assigned to her, but most of all, she was reliable and trustworthy. As a young professional and educated woman, she felt entitled to a particular lifestyle, but working for Darren was not the best way to attain it, so she thought. She initially thought there would be a lot of bartering when she barged into Darren's office to demand a ten thousand- dollar raise, but to her surprise, Darren offered her a twelve-thousand dollar raise based on her performance. Abigail had earned every penny. She didn't know what to say when he agreed to her demands and more. She felt a little awkward walking out of the office afterwards. Whatever fight she had in her when she first walked into Darren's office, vanished when he flashed his smile and told her he was giving her an even bigger raise. For that act of kindness, Abigail decided to treat Darren to lunch.

She called the Chinese restaurant and had them deliver a Pu Pu platter with every imaginable available Chinese dish from the restaurant. There were chicken wings, boneless spare ribs, egg rolls, chicken fingers, beef teriyaki, fried wontons, crab Rangoon, fried shrimp and a side order of shrimp fried rice. Abigail went all out for her boss. Twelve thousand dollars was gonna go a long way for her. There was so much food; neither Darren nor Abigail could eat it all.

Darren smiled when Abigail knocked on his door with a food tray sitting on her hands. He quickly got up and cleared a portion of his conference table, so she could set the tray down. "Is today a special occasion or something? That's a lot of food, and all my favorites," he blurted out. "Well, since my boss was kind of enough to give me a handsome raise today, I want to be kind and treat him to lunch," she said in a somewhat flirtatious way. "I hope you didn't spend your entire raise on this food," Darren joked. "You are so funny, your wife must be the luckiest woman in the world," she told him. "Can I call her, so you can remind her please?" he joked. Laughter invaded the room before they took their seats at the table and started grubbing.

On this particular Friday, Abigail seemed a little more flirtatious than usual. Since she had become a good assistant to Darren, the borders opened up just a little more than before and she was able to cross the line sometimes. "How's everything at home with Tina?" she asked with curiosity in her voice, while slowly running her tongue across her luscious lips. The sexual innuendo was obvious, but Darren downplayed it. "My wife is great. She's always great. I don't know what I'd do without her," he responded. It wasn't exactly the answer that Abigail was looking for, but it was what she got. Abigail often wore jeans on casual Fridays, but on this particular Friday, her jeans were especially tight. A man is gonna be a man and Darren was not to blame for noticing Abigail's perfect ass. He glanced once or twice throughout the day, but that was the end of it.

In between bites, Abigail and Darren discussed their weekend plans and she revealed to him she was single. He couldn't believe a woman as fine as her was single. "How does a woman as fine as you stay single in a city like New York?" Darren curiously asked. "It's by choice. I have my type and I'm not going to settle. I usually get what I want, so I'd rather wait for him," she said with a grin. "Well, if you're interested, I have a wonderful person that I would like to introduce you to. He's a wonderful guy who happens to be single and looking for a wonderful woman," Darren offered. "That sounds good and all, but whenever I hear the word wonderful when someone is describing a friend, I get chills all over my body, because that usually means the person is not that attractive," she said without interest. "On the contrary, Will is a great looking guy and a wonderful human being," Darren chimed. "If he's so good looking and wonderful, why is he single?" she asked. "Actually, the same can be said about you, wouldn't you agree?" Darren asked. Abigail shook her head when she realized she had just put her foot in her mouth. The two of them finished their lunch and it was time to get back to work. Darren got up to walk back towards his desk, while Abigail cleaned the table. She stared at him with hungry eyes momentarily as he moved around his office, but Darren wasn't paying her any attention.

At the end of the work day, Darren did something that he hadn't done in the past, he asked Abigail to call him over the weekend if she was interested in meeting Will. Sure, Abigail always had Darren's number for emergency use only, but not for anything personal. Abigail was ecstatic, not because of the prospect of meeting Will, but because she would get an opportunity to talk to Darren over the weekend. It appeared Abigail had made up her mind as to whom she wanted her man to be, but that would only happen over Tina's dead body.

Chapter 9

Darren and Tina were out running their usual errands when his phone rang. On Saturdays, the two of them usually went food shopping together. Tina would come home and do the laundry while Darren would help clean the house. It was a mutual arrangement and the two of them enjoyed helping each other out around the house. Darren and Tina were still at the supermarket when Abigail's number and name popped up on his telephone screen as it rang. "Hey, what's up?" Darren said, trying not to alert Tina. "Hi boss. I'm calling to see about that hook up with your brother in-law," Abigail said in her most seductive voice. Darren pulled the phone from his ear for a second and said in his head, 'this woman's tripping with all that sexiness on the phone.' When he brought the phone back to his ear, he said, "So you're interested in meeting Will?" There was momentary silence as if Darren's question had tripped her. "Of course, you said he was a nice guy. However, I would be more comfortable meeting him with you around," she said. Darren shook his head, because he didn't understand why a grown woman needed his presence to feel comfortable with another man, but he shrugged it off. "Well, I haven't talked to my wife about it yet to see if it's a good idea, but I'll get back to you after I get her feedback on it," he said trying to rush her off the phone. "You sound like you're busy, do you need to go?" she asked, hoping his answer would be to her advantage. "Actually, my wife and I are at the supermarket doing some food shopping. I will give you a call later," he told her. "Well, ok. Bye, Darren," she said, trying to sound sexy again. Darren shook his head as he caught up with his wife who was in the produce section looking at different fruits and vegetables.

"Babe, you know who just called me?" Darren asked his wife to see her reaction. "No, but I'm sure you're gonna tell me," Tina said. That was Darren's way of getting rid of his guilt. "It was Abigail. I vaguely mentioned to her yesterday that I would introduce her to Will, since she's single and all and with his recent break up, he needs to meet somebody nice," Darren told Tina. "How you know she's single? Is that what y'all talk about all day in the office? Aren't you getting a too little personal with your assistant?" she said, as she rolled her eyes. Darren didn't know how to react. She waited to see his face turn color before she said, "Psych! I got you. You should see your face right now." Darren breathed a sigh of relief when Tina revealed she was only playing with him. "I think her and Will would make a nice couple. She seems nice and she's pretty, which is one of the major requirements for Will," Tina said with a little attitude, to add effect to her statement. Darren was glad that his wife thought his suggestion was good. "When is Will gonna be in town again?" he asked. "Well, you know the sorry Falcons never make it past the first round in the playoffs, anyway. So he should be home in a couple of weeks," Tina said. "That's wrong, Tina. You shouldn't be talking about your brother's team like that," Darren said trying to tease his wife. "It's the truth, though. It ain't like it's Will's fault they don't make it past the first round in the playoffs. He always plays his ass off, but everybody else is always coming up short," she said through laughter. "You are one mean sister. I hope you don't be dogging me like that when I'm not around," Darren said playfully. "I can't do that to you. You're my husband and you're a reflection of me. Besides, with a woman like me by your side, you never have to worry about failing. I got your back, babe," she said before moving in for a peck on the lips. "That's right! My baby's got my back, and baby got back, too. I wanna take some of that back when we get home," he said, while looking at his wife with hungry eyes. "Come on then. You know you ain't gotta tell me twice. Let's hurry up with this shopping," Tina said with excitement in her voice.

Darren and Tina hurried back home for another one of their steamy sessions, but it was all interrupted when Will called Tina to check up on her. Tina almost didn't pick up the phone when she glanced at the screen and noticed her brother's name flashing while it rang. "It's Will. I have to pick it up. He might have an emergency," she told Darren as his dick was deep in her trenches. "Hello," she said after finally picking up on the fourth ring. "Am I interrupting something? It took you forever to answer the phone. I can call back," Will told his sister. "No, it's okay, Will," Tina managed to say, while her eyes rolled in the back of her head under the sweetness of Darren's slow strokes. Tina may have been interrupted by the phone, but Darren was trying to keep his stride. Tina's legs were spread wide as Darren slowly mashed up her sweet pussy. She couldn't help grinding on his hard dick, while listening to her brother on the phone. "I was just calling to let you know that I will be in New York next weekend, so you can plan on spending some time with your brother," Will told her. "That's good, Will. Darren and I have someone we'd like to introduce you to," she let him know. "Yeah, is it for business or personal?" Will asked with curiosity. "It all depends, but she's right up your alley," Tina said muffling her words. "You don't sound like yourself, sis. I think I caught you in a compromising situation. You and Darren never let up. I'm gonna let you go. I'll see you next week. Love you," Will told his sister. "You know me a little too well. Love you too. Bye." Tina hung up the phone and refocused her energy on the Mandingo who was working hard on satisfying her needs.

Tina's fingers were digging into the sheet and her teeth found comfort in the pillow as Darren reconstructed her pipeline with some of his best strokes. "Fuck me hard, baby. I want it rough," Tina told Darren. It wasn't unusual for Tina to beg Darren to punish her with his huge cock. Sometimes rough sex was the only thing that could satisfy her. Darren held on to her shoulders as he unleashed his punishing strokes in the depth of Tina's sugar wall. The grimace on Tina's face confirmed the pleasure-pain she was under, but she kept begging for more. "That's it, baby. Fuck your pussy hard. Make me feel it," she begged. Darren was fucking Tina with all his might. She raised her ass up, so all twelve hard inches of Darren's dick could reach her bottom. "Yes, fill that pussy with your dick!" she yelled. Darren was motivated and he fulfilled her highness' request. Adding to her pleasure, Darren started smacking Tina's ass hard. The sting of his fingers across her skin was ecstasy to her. "That's it, baby. Smack my ass hard. I wanna cum for you," she announced. Darren grabbed her left ass cheek with his left hand, while smacking the right one with his right hand, never losing his stride. The harder his strokes, the closer Tina came to climax. It took just a few more strokes before Tina started shaking violently, as sweat covered her face. "I'm cumming, baby! I'm cumming. Don't stop!" she begged as Darren made her cum once more.

Chapter 10

Darren went back to work that Monday morning with some exciting news for Abigail. He couldn't wait to tell her that Will was going to be in town the upcoming weekend. He felt she deserved someone in her life that could make her happy. Things didn't work out with Cassandra and Will because he started to think she was a little too overbearing and wanted to control every aspect of his life, including his finances. He misread her completely. She wanted to protect him, because everyone around him and every organization were reaching out to Will for a handout all the time. His mom, dad and sister were the only people who genuinely care for him, Cassandra believed. He didn't know how to say no to people. She wanted to step in and control that. The transformation Will noticed in Cassandra also changed him. He was apprehensive about women and relationships altogether. Sweet Cassandra turned out to be a control freak, according to Will. He was distraught when the relationship ended, but it was all his own doing. As a single professional athlete, he went back to bedding as many groupies as he could possibly find in Atlanta. Will knew they wanted nothing more than money from him. He had become desensitized to his emotions for women. However, he had also started to feel like a lame. He wanted someone special in his life, but that would prove easier said than done in Georgia. Will's status and visibility as a player in the league increased. Most of the money-hungry groupies knew of his generous heart. Often times, he couldn't differentiate between the real women and the fake ones. He just went with the flow and eventually figured who the predators were a little too late.   Darren was hoping he could shake things up for Will in a positive way. Though he and Will didn't talk regularly, Tina kept him abreast with what was going on in Will's life. Will didn't want to wait until he retired from the league to get married. He wanted his wife home with him by the time he retired, but he was not having much luck meeting anyone special. Maybe his luck was about to change in New York, he thought.

Abigail strolled into the office at 8:45 AM as usual. That particular morning, she was dressed excessively sexy. She wore a tight gray mini skirt, a white fitted long sleeved shirt that accentuated her curvaceous body, a long coat and four-inch high heel pumps. The reveal was breathtaking for Darren. It had been awhile since Abigail had exposed her exotic curves in the office. Since that conversation with Darren about the inappropriateness of her outfit, Abigail walked a straight line and did everything in her power to dress professionally without offending Darren. "You look especially nice today. Do you have a hot date?" Darren asked after Abigail walked into his office to greet him. "As a matter of fact, I do. I have a dinner date after work today, but I wouldn't make too much of it for now," she revealed. Maybe Abigail was using a new strategy to get away with wearing something nice and sexy every now and then in the office, but Darren took her at her words. "Where'd you meet this lucky fellow?" Darren asked interestingly enough. "I went to this spot in Manhattan over the weekend with my girlfriend and I met this guy. We talked a few times over the phone and he invited me to dinner tonight," she revealed. Abigail could sense that Darren was admiring her outfit and perhaps her curves. She knew the stance she needed to take to get his full attention. Being a little bow-legged worked to Abigail's advantage. Abigail stood in front of Darren with her legs spread like a wishbone under her skirt with the backdrop of the sun through the open shades on the window, which created a sequence of nothingness. Darren could mold a cast of Abigail's shape if he wanted to, it was hard to resist. He quickly turned his head as her form came into view when stepped right in the path of the bright sun, pussy lips hanging from her thong and all. It was no longer imagination. The light from the sun cut right through Abigail's skirt and Darren had to catch himself before revealing himself accidentally. His dick shot right up. He had a man moment.

Looking away from Abigail's silhouette in the sun, Darren asked, "Where are you guys going for dinner?" Abigail noticed the effect she had on Darren right away. She ran her hand through her hair in the most seductive way and said, "He's taking me to Havana Central restaurant in Manhattan." Though Abigail didn't notice the erection growing in Darren's pants under his desk, Darren felt ashamed and uncomfortable for allowing himself to get a hard-on for his assistant. He stayed behind the desk to shield his crotch from Abigail's view, but he knew he couldn't just go on as if this transformation didn't take place. Darren found Abigail attractive, but he would never cheat on Tina. At least that's what he wanted to believe at the time. "You guys are gonna have Cuban food? That's good. Tina and I go to this nice Cuban restaurant in Manhattan called, Café Cortadito, all the time. You're gonna love the food," he told her. "I'm looking forward to it. I've never had Cuban food before," she said.

Darren had completely forgotten to mention to Abigail that Will was coming to town for the weekend. He spent most of the day in his office, avoiding contact with Abigail as much as possible. Working in a small office with an attractive woman was becoming a difficult task, and Darren didn't want to jeopardize his marriage at the expense of a cheap thrill. Tina was the love of his life and it was going to remain that way. Much of what Darren had to do that day happened at his desk. He did not want to lay eyes on Abigail. He breathed a sigh of relief when the day finally ended and she went about her merry way. Darren hoped that Abigail only dressed so seductively because she had a date. He wished to see a professionally dressed Abigail in looser clothes for the rest of the week. Though her outfit was corporately acceptable, Darren wanted to tell her to tone it down a bit.

It wasn't until four days later that Tina reminded Darren that Will was coming to town, and asked if he had told Abigail about him. "You know what? It completely slipped my mind, babe. I'll have to remember to tell her in the morning," he told his wife. That night, there was no humping, winding or grinding; Tina and Darren called it an early night. They were both exhausted from a long day.

Darren showed up the next morning to find Abigail had already opened the office. She was jovial, as usual. She made sure she got Darren his morning coffee and a Danish from Dunkin Donuts. She left them on his desk. He was pleasantly surprised when he walked in his office to find what she had done. "You seem to be in a great mood this morning, what's going on?" he asked. "Nothing spectacular, I just want to show my gratitude to you and I wanna appreciate my life," she announced. "That reminds me, my brother-in-law is coming to town this weekend... would you like to join us for dinner? I know you mentioned you'd be more comfortable meeting him if I were around," Darren reminded her. "Sure. I would love to meet him. I hope he's as handsome as my boss," she said jokingly. "The ladies seem to think he's a good looking guy. Don't worry, you'll like him," Darren assured her. "Where are we going?" she asked with curiosity. "We're just gonna have a nice dinner at my house. It's been a while since we've seen Will. I also figure the casual environment will take the pressure off you guys," Darren told her. "Remind me to give you my address before you leave tonight," Darren told casually. "I'm looking forward to it," she said with a smile across her face. "Is there any particular dish that you like?" Darren asked. "I'm not a picky eater. I'll try almost anything," she revealed. Needless to say, the rest of the day went well.

By day's end, Abigail reminded Darren to write down his address on a piece of paper and the time to show up for dinner. Abigail was overly excited. She had never been to Darren's house and didn't even know where he lived. He kept his private life separate from his work, but he was about to open Pandora's box and see a new side of Abigail he had never seen before.

Chapter 11

Dinner was scheduled for six o'clock on Saturday evening. The table was nicely arranged and Will was anticipating the arrival of Abigail. He knew his sister wouldn't pick a bad looking woman for him and Darren assured him in so many words, without offending his wife, Abigail was fine. Will was excited about the possibility of meeting someone new who might be good for him. Everyone was sitting in the living room waiting for Abigail to arrive. She showed up just a couple of minutes after 6:00 pm. Abigail's outfit was jaw-dropping, as she removed her long light brown suede coat. It wasn't so much that her dress was sexy, but the fact that her body made the dress looked so damn good. She wore a tan, fitted long-sleeved, turtleneck sweater dress made of cashmere. The dress barely rested above her knees and she wore a nice pair of four-inch, knee-high light brown suede boots that matched her light brown coat. She looked incredible. Will was almost rude the way he stared at her body without acknowledging her presence when she extended her hand to shake his, when they were being introduced. "I'm sorry, but you are drop-dead gorgeous," Will said without realizing the words had escaped his mouth, while shaking Abigail's hand. Darren had a look of shock on his face, too, but he quickly wiped it away when his wife turned to see his reaction to Abigail's dress. Tina was never the type of woman to feel threatened by another woman, but Abigail forced her to quickly think about a threesome in the moment, even if it was temporary.

She looked good enough for men and women to be jealous of her. "I am Abigail. You must be Will," she said as Will continued to admire her. "Welcome to our home," Tina said as she directed Abigail towards the living room with her hand. "Thanks for having me," Abigail replied. "Don't worry about Will, he'll calm down in a few minutes. You'd think he'd be used to beautiful women by now, as much as they chase after him," Tina revealed. Abigail laughed timidly at Tina's comments about her brother. "I don't know if Darren told you, but my brother is a starting linebacker for the Atlanta Falcons. He's not just handsome, he's talented as well, and rich," she said with pride. Abigail thought Will was cute, but he wasn't her usual type. She could work with him, she figured, but the real prize was the forbidden fruit sitting across the table wearing a light blue v-neck sweater and a gray pair of slacks with black shoes and belt to match. Darren's defined chest could be seen through his sweater and Abigail inconspicuously peeked at him ever chance she got.

Meanwhile, Will tried to make small talk with Abigail at the table while Darren opened a bottle of red wine. "Where are you from?" Will asked. Abigail's eyes were piercing and Will almost got lost in them. She stared straight into his face, almost with a look of disinterest and said, "I'm originally from Jamaica, Queens, but I live in Elmont now." She followed with a smile. That smile gave Will more hope than she could've imagined. Not only that, it also lit up the whole room. Abigail's perfect teeth and smile was one of her best assets, however, it also became a kryptonite to Will as he tried too hard to gain Abigail's attention. For a minute, Will thought she acted like she was not interested in him because his sister had mentioned the beautiful groupies he was always surrounded by, but that wasn't the case at all, Abigail just wasn't interested in Will period. Still, she was polite towards him and made it clear to him that she wasn't interested in a long distance relationship with a professional athlete. Darren didn't understand why she agreed to meet Will if she wasn't interested in dating an athlete who lived out of town. And then he thought about the fact that she'd had a date earlier in the week with another guy, and maybe things were moving along well for her with the guy. It was no sweat to him, because he knew Will was a good guy who would eventually find the right woman that fit his lifestyle.

Tina did a great job, pulling all the stops to prepare a wonderful dinner. For dinner, she served buttermilk biscuits, cornbread, chopped salad, scalloped potatoes, baked savory rice, old fashioned beef pot roast, southern fried chicken and macaroni and cheese. For dessert, she served midnight velvet chocolate cake and cheesecake. She knew her brother could eat enough for three people, so she made plenty of food. Tina had been sharpening her cooking skills since she got married. One of her favorite pastimes was cooking dinner for her husband. Dinner was delicious and everyone was satisfied. For a fit woman, Abigail could throw down. She sampled almost every dish on the table, and was impressed by Tina's cooking skills. "You're gonna have to teach me how to make some of these dishes. Your food is good," she said, while wiping her mouth lightly with a napkin. "She knew her big brother was coming and know how I get down," said Will, while rubbing his belly to get a smile out of everyone. It worked. Abigail smiled at him and gave him the 'you're kind of cute' eye. Will was keeping hope alive. Abigail hadn't really taken inventory of Will's attire since she came in. It wasn't until he got up she noticed that he shopped at the Big and Tall store. He had no choice, Will's a big guy. He wasn't trendy enough for her taste and she had made up her mind that she could only keep him as a friend. Will was too big a guy for her. However, like most women, Abigail was also taking inventory of Tina's outfit and her beauty. Tina looked gorgeous as usual in her knee-high black suede boots, short black miniskirt and a cream cashmere sweater. Abigail stared at her with envy.

    After dinner, Abigail offered to help Tina tidy up the kitchen, as Darren and Will moved to the family room to watch ESPN. "You know I'll be more than happy to wash the dishes and clean up, babe," Darren told his wife before making his way towards the family room. At the same time, Will made his way to the fridge to grab a six-pack of Heineken to bring to the family room with him. "I got this, babe. You can go and watch your game with Will in the family room," she said. "Yeah, we got this," Abigail chimed in. Tina smiled at her. "I would offer my help, but you know I can't wash no dishes. Besides, my maid does all my house work. I work too hard during the season to come home and have to wash dishes. Hell naw!" said Will, creating more distance between he and Abigail, without realizing it. Abigail thought it was sweet of Darren to offer to help. He was caring and sweet, she thought. Will seemed a little arrogant to her, but that had become part of his nature because of the brutal sport he played. He had to display confidence and sometimes arrogance to instill fear in his opponents. It was all good-natured, but Abigail didn't know him well enough to see it that way.

Will and Darren were in the family room for a couple of hours before Tina and Abigail emerged. They both seemed a little tipsy as they finished off the bottle of wine. Darren and Will had been drinking the six-pack of Heineken that Will had retrieved from the fridge, and had a little buzz of their own. Tina became a little more flirtatious with her husband in the presence of company. Though Will was used to Tina's flirtatious and loving behavior towards her husband, Abigail just laughed it off. The four of them sat in the family room to watch the Boston Celtics put a spanking on their loving New York Knickerbockers. By the time the game was over, Abigail's buzz had worn off and she was ready to drive back home. "I had a wonderful evening with all of you. I hope we can do it again soon," she said as she got up to get ready to go. Will stood up from his seat as well. "Abigail, are you available for dinner tomorrow?" Will asked confidently without worrying about the response he might get from Abigail. "Will, I'm sure you're a wonderful man, but I don't want to lead you on. It's too much drama to deal with a professional athlete, especially a handsome one at that," she said in an attempt to stroke his ego. Big Will felt a little less embarrassed because she found him attractive. "I understand. Don't worry about it. It was nice meeting you, anyway," said Will before setting back down to take a seat on the couch. Abigail would remain the fish that got away from Will.

Chapter 12

Will spent a week in New York visiting family and his friends. He had plenty of fun hanging around with his buddies, giving them VIP access everywhere they went. Whenever they were out, his friends also benefited with the ladies because he was an NFL player. Will knew how to put the "F" in fun. While Will may have been a little too carefree or nonchalant about those around him, his sister constantly reminded him he was no longer a regular Joe and he had to be careful who he hung around with. One guy in particular that Tina wanted her brother to keep away from was this dude named Eddie. He was known as fast Eddie because he got his way with the women very fast back in high school. It didn't take long for him to sleep with the girls back then. He would walk around school and brag about all the women he slept with. Fast Eddie was a former football player who played football with Will in high school, but his aspiration of becoming a professional football player was cut short when he blew his ACL and his MCL during his sophomore year in college. Fast Eddie attempted, but he never truly recovered from his injuries. He also became depressed. By the time he emerged from his depression, he no longer knew how to cope as a regular person. He was accustomed to star treatment most of his life, so it was the only way to live, according to him. Eddie would go through any length to remain a star. Though his glory days were behind him, Eddie remained a star in his own mind.

Shortly after Will left to return back to Atlanta, a woman named him as the perpetrator in a sexual assault case. When Tina saw the story on the news, she quickly called her brother to have a talk with him. The phone rang endlessly before Will finally picked up. "Hello," he said, almost out of breath. Tina could hear the moaning and groaning of the woman in the background. "Fuck me, Will," the woman could be heard whispering in the background through the phone. "Maybe this is the wrong time to talk, but I'm gonna need you to call me back ASAP when you're done with your little skank," Tina said angrily. Will couldn't understand why his sister was so pissed, but his nut was nearing and he had to finish what he started. "Lift your leg up and place it on the nightstand," Will ordered the tiny 5ft 3-inch tall woman to do. She obliged, exposing her pinkness for Will to crush with force. Will stared at himself in the mirror sitting on the dresser across the room as he stroked the beautiful young woman's pussy. "Yes! Fuck me!" she kept screaming as Will stung her ass with his thick fingers. "Spank me, daddy!" she yelled. Will's condom was starting to become dry, but he had to bust that nut. "Oh shit, here it comes!" he announced. "Cum for me, daddy" she said. Will grabbed her ass tightly and released himself in the condom inside her. Sweat covered his body like he had just experienced heat exhaustion on the practice field. "That was good, baby," she complimented him. "I'm gonna need you to get dressed and go home, because I have to take care a few things. I'll holler at you later," Will told her. "Ok," she said as she picked up some money from the nightstand and her clothing on the floor as she walked towards the bathroom to freshen up. Will grabbed a robe from his closet and waited for the woman to leave before dialing his sister's number. "I'll see you later," she said before walking out the door to her car. "See you," Will responded without as much as giving her a kiss or a hug. It was purely a sexual relationship.

Will sat on his bed and dialed Tina's number. The phone rang twice before Tina picked up. "Hello, what the hell is wrong you!" she shouted through the phone. "What's the matter?" Will asked calmly. "What's the matter? Your ass is all over the news because some white chick is claiming you sexually assaulted. There's a warrant out for your arrest, Will. You're gonna need a lawyer. Did your agent call you to make you aware of this?" Tina asked with frustration in her voice. "T, I know you don't believe I assaulted some white girl, right?" he asked, hoping to get reassurance from his sister. "I know your ass ain't crazy enough to do no dumb shit like that, but I also told you to watch the people around you. These leeches don't give a shit about you, they just wanna spend your money," she said angrily. "T, everything's gonna be all right. I didn't have sex with anybody while I was in New York. I went out with Fast Eddie and 'em, but I didn't touch none of the girls in that suite," he revealed. "Suite? What suite?" Tina asked. Will had to recollect his thoughts before answering her question. "One of the nights when I was out with the guys, these women we met at the club wanted to leave with us, so I got us a suite in Manhattan just to hang out. One of the white girl's gave me head, but that was it. We didn't do anything else. Fast Eddie can vouch for that," he told her with confidence. "Fast Eddie? You trust that low down dirty bastard? Fast Eddie was always jealous of you, why would you even be hanging with him?" Tina asked angrily. "T, that was some high school shit. We moved past that. He came along because I invited the other guys to come out to the club with me," Will told her. "Will, you have got to remember you're not a regular citizen. You're a millionaire athlete, which makes you a target for everybody who's looking to run a scam. I'm tired of telling you to be careful," Tina said with sadness in her voice. "Does mom and dad know?" Will asked hesitantly. "They don't know now, but they will once they get home. It's all over the news, and I'm sure it will be on CNN soon enough, so you can see it in Atlanta for yourself." Tina was frustrated and mad at her brother for allowing himself to get into such a compromising situation. "T, I have to go. I'm gonna call my agent to see if I can get a lawyer to get me out of this bullshit," Will said before hanging up the phone. He didn't know the severity of the case yet.

After getting off the phone with his sister, Will grabbed the remote control off the mantle to turn on his flat-screen television that hung on the wall. After switching the channel to CNN, he plopped down on his bed in frustration. Five minutes later, the anchor came on to announce, "Breaking news! Atlanta Falcons linebacker, William Stevens, is being sought in connection of a sexual assault in New York City. The assault allegedly took place at the Beekman Tower hotel in Manhattan. The victim, Amy Geller, alleges that Mr. Stevens forced her into oral sex and she filed a police report at the station in Manhattan. A warrant has been issued for the arrest of Mr. Stevens who is now considered a fugitive from the law." Will shook his head and couldn't believe it. There was no time for a breather as his agent called him to find out what the hell was going on. Will tried to explain to his agent that the story about him on TV wasn't true. "Look, man, I went out with a group of friends and rented a two-bedroom suite at a hotel in Manhattan because my friends wanted to keep the party going after the club. We invited these chicks to come back with us and that's all that happened." There was a long silent pause on the phone. His agent was trying to figure out the best way to approach the situation. "Are you sure, Will? You can't leave out any details that's gonna rip holes in your story. We need to be consistent with our statement and I'm gonna get you the best lawyer to fight these charges," his agent assured him. Will's agent had been with him since he was drafted, so he knew Will's character. "I'll tell you exactly what happened. There were five of us hanging out that night, including myself in the VIP section at the club. We were drinking, partying, and having a good time. One of my friends decided to go out into the crowd to get some women. He brought back a bevy of young women willing to party the night away with us in the VIP section. There must've been at least five or six women that came back with him. Bottles were popping and everyone agreed we would continue the party after the club, but I couldn't bring them back to my parents' house, so I decided to get a hotel suite. I called around to see if I could find a hotel with a suite in Manhattan, which I did. My friends and I drove straight from the club to the hotel with the women in tow, following us in their own car. When we got there, the women started getting buck wild, but this particular woman named Amy had her eyes on me. She took me away from the crowd, into the other bedroom in the suite, so we could talk in private. All I intended to do was to talk to her, but she wasn't trying to hear that." His agent listened intently before asking, "What do you mean she wasn't trying to hear that?" Will was almost embarrassed, but he had to tell his agent what truly happened in order to keep his ass from going to prison for sexual assault.

It took a little contemplating, but Will's agent was able to convince him to finish the story and promised that it would be kept confidential between them and the attorney. "The minute I got in the room, Amy, I believe that was her name, had other plans. She went straight for my crotch. She unzipped my pants and took my dick in her mouth. When I asked her what she was doing? She answered, 'what do you think I'm doing? I'm about to give you the blowjob of your life.' You know I couldn't punk out from getting a blowjob. She sucked me off until I came in her mouth, and that was it. We went back to join the other people in the other room until the party ended a few minutes later. A couple of my friends slept in the other room and on the sofa, while I slept in the second bedroom alone. The girl was long gone, along with the other women and Fast Eddie." The agent didn't say too much other than a statement needed to be made to the media and he would get the attorney on it as soon as possible.

While Will's agent was thinking about damage control, Will was losing his mind because he couldn't believe he had been so careless. He was one of a few NFL players with absolutely no blemish on his records, whatsoever. He prided himself for being careful and amounted his good behavior to the great job his parents did raising him. Sports analysts often referred to Will as "the Clean-cut Linebacker." He was the big teddy bear who did his job without causing any raucous for anyone in the Falcons organization and the league. Now, Will worried that his reputation would take a tumble and his image would be down the tubes. Endorsers started calling his agents to drop him until further notice. Not only was this incident hurting his image, it was also hurting his pockets. The next thing to do was for Will to fly up to New York to turn himself in to the NYPD. After surrendering at the station with his lawyer by his side, Will was handcuffed and placed in a cell. A few hours went by before he was taken down to the courthouse for a bail hearing. Because Will was a millionaire, he had to surrender his passport, even though he wasn't a flight risk. He posted bond at two million dollars, while his mother wept in the courtroom. She couldn't believe that her son had fallen victim to the traps set for most athletes by women. His father was stoic in court and confidently believed that his son was innocent.

After Will was released, he left the court with his parents through a back door and they drove straight to Long Island to their home, escaping the hoopla with all the reporters waiting in front of the courthouse to question Will about his guilt or innocence. On the ride to the house, Will explained the whole thing to his parents, but his mother was worried that his high profile image would create bias in the public's eye and he might not get a fair shake in court. She was silently praying for her son, while holding tight to his hand. Will needed all the comfort he could get at the time. His father was silent during the whole ride.

Meanwhile, the white neighbors on Will's block were ready to sell their homes, because they didn't want a sexual predator living on their street. These people knew Will since he was a kid. It was a matter of time before something happened to the only black family in their upper-middleclass neighborhood. Will's mom wasn't trying to let them treat her son any old way. She had no problem brandishing her revolver that everyone on that street knew she carried at all times. If anybody messed with her boy, she would let them have it. These white folks knew better.

Chapter 13

Darren was almost embarrassed when he had to go back to his office the next day after the incident with Will was all over the news, and knew he had to face Abigail. He didn't know how she felt, but the media made it sound as if Will was guilty in the court of opinion. However, Abigail was more impartial than Darren believed. It was sullen in the office that day. Darren wasn't his jovial self and Abigail didn't do much to engage him. She went about her day and accomplished only the tasks she was supposed to do at work. Finally, the silence was killing her and she had to say something to Darren about the situation. She knocked on his door and waited for him to invite her in, something she seldom did before, but Darren understood. "Come in," he said when he heard her knock. Abigail looked great as usual, but Darren's mind was somewhere else. Will was facing some serious charges that could potentially end his career with the NFL, and it bothered him. He waited for Abigail to speak. She looked at him and smiled, before opening her mouth and said, "For what it's worth, I think your brother-in-law is a nice guy and I don't think he did what that white woman is accusing him of." It was almost like weight had been lifted off Darren's shoulders, but he wanted to concur her feelings. "Will is just not that type of guy. I know this woman is lying, but he has to prove that it didn't go down as she said. Will is one of the nicest people I know and he would never take advantage of a woman. That's just not his style," he told Abigail. "I could sense that," Abigail said for assurance. The day was coming to an end and she was ready to leave, anyway. "Well, I'm gonna head home now. I'll see you tomorrow, boss," she said, while smiling at Darren. "It's five o'clock already? This day just flew by. Have a good evening and get home safe," he said to her before she walked out of his office.

Darren was letting Will's situation distract him a little too much. Will had become the brother he never had and the two of them enjoyed the relationship they shared. When Darren got home that evening, he turned his television to ESPN, because he was tired of all the sensationalism associated with the case. However, no sooner did he turn the channel to ESPN's Sportcenter, the sports anchor, Stan Verett, announced, "We're gonna take you live to a press conference being held by Atlanta Falcons linebacker, William Stevens, and his attorney." Darren just shook his head and waited for the camera to cut to the press conference. Will was accompanied by his attorney and agent as he head read his statement, "Today is a very sad day in my NFL career. I just want to reiterate that at no point in time did I ever force myself on anybody. The evidence will prove in a court of law that everything that took place that night was consensual and I never assaulted anybody in any way. I'm innocent of these frivolous charges and I will fight hard to restore my great reputation as one of the most respected players in the NFL. I will be exonerated of all these charges in a court of law. Thanks for your time." There were hundreds of reporter standings around waiting to ask questions, but to their disappointment, Will's attorney announced, "We will not be taking any questions at this time. Thank you very much for your time." The reporters were left to speculate and that's what most of them did over the next few months.

Darren hadn't talked to Will since he went back to Atlanta and he wanted to reserve any judgment or opinion on the case. He got bits and pieces of the story from his wife, but she was always emotional when she told him whatever it was that she knew. He also didn't want to put Will in a compromising position, but he knew that Will needed as much support as possible at the time. Calling Will to check up on him was the only he could do, however, before he could pick up the phone to place the call, another story was running on ESPN. "Breaking news! The Falcons have just announced the indefinite suspension of linebacker, William Stevens, from the team until further notice," Stan Verett announced on the air. That was just the beginning of a catastrophic moment in Will's career. The NFL has always made it difficult to throw their support behind players who face sexual assault charges, and with the recent killings of players' wives and other assault cases in the media, the Falcons needed to make a statement. The mounting pressure coming from feminist groups only added to pressure to Falcons personnel to make the decision that they made. Things weren't looking up for Will at all. One mistake of partying with the wrong crowd for one night could possibly cost Will his career, Darren thought.

Darren knew all the hoopla going on in the media had to be eating at Will. He picked up the phone and dialed Will's number. He waited patiently as he formed his thoughts before speaking to Will. The phone rang for a while, as the media had been trying to reach out to Will for a statement, any statement. He wanted so much to defend himself, but under the advice of his lawyer, he couldn't say anything. "Hello," Will answered the phone with relief in his voice as he noticed Darren's name flashing across the screen. "What's going on, Will? I'm calling to check up on you, to make sure everything is ok," Darren said. "What's up, Darren? I'm good, man, but I've seen better days," he said. "I know, man. I can understand what you're going through right now," Darren tried to console him. "These people are trying to destroy a career that I worked hard to build, man. I don't get this, man. I can't believe how the media can just turn on me like that just because some white chick made up a story about me assaulting her," Will sounded a little delusional to have trusted the media to begin with. "I'm sure you will pull through this and everything will be all right," Darren told him. Will appreciated the vote of confidence from Darren. He went on to explain everything that happened in the hotel room that night to Darren. Will had been a recluse because he wanted to avoid situations like these, but nobody can lock themselves in the house forever, Darren thought.

It was a hard way to learn a lesson, but Will was finding out the price of fame and his extraordinary talent was a double edge sword. The leeches were always waiting in line for the next opportunity and Will was blindsided by something he never saw coming. However, the true story would unfold in the media just months after the initial incident.

Chapter 14

Meanwhile, Darren still had a business to run and life went on. Though Darren was bothered by Will's situation, he couldn't neglect his clients. As Will's financial life took a tumble, Darren wanted to make sure his assets were intact, as well as his investments, at least the ones he had access to, anyway. Around the office, Abigail picked up whatever slack Darren was experiencing. Tina was starting to worry a lot about the possibility of her brother's freedom being taken away. She would call Darren at the office for comfort, but most of the time he was too busy with his work to spend too much time on the phone with his wife. However, Tina found comfort from a source she never imagined. Abigail was more than willing to hear Tina's pain and her fear about the status of her brother. Darren was even a little happy that his wife and Abigail were finally connecting. He dismissed the daily long talks between Abigail and Tina as the bonding of two girlfriends establishing a new relationship. In more ways than one, Abigail had taken a burden away from Darren. Tina used to come to him with all her problems, and sometimes he just didn't want to be bothered.

The New Year had come and gone and Darren and Tina didn't celebrate much. Will had a hearing scheduled for mid March and the family couldn't wait to learn Will's fate. The anticipation of what was to come brought the family closer. Everyone tried their best to keep Will's spirit up, but he remained in Atlanta where he called home, alone.

Will's case had become the dominating topic in Atlanta and on ESPN. He couldn't hide from it. However, the over-sensationalism of the case also brought back a familiar person into Will's life. Though Will and Cassandra had parted ways, she still cared enough about him to extend her support to him. She had dated Will long enough to know that he wasn't the monster that the media was making him out to be. Besides, she was still in love with him and his big heart. She wanted him to know that there were people in his life who still cared about him, and she was one of them.

The phone rang four times before Will apprehensively picked it up. One more ring would've sent it to his voicemail, or Cassandra would've hung up. She wasn't in the mood to leave him a voicemail. She wanted to talk to him, to comfort him and let him know everything was going to be okay. "Hello," said Will hesitantly through the Bluetooth, while he lay on his couch watching one of his favorite movies, *Do The Right Thing*. The pleasantry in Cassandra's tone brought a changing effect to Will's mood. "You know I've missed you so much, but I also know that you may need some support right now," Cassandra said to Will after hearing his voice. "Baby?" Will questioned with hope in his voice. "Yes. It's me," Cassandra said without realizing how much light she had brought to Will's day. "Baby, I'm sorry about everything." Will went into an apologetic frenzy, but Cassandra stopped him in his track. "We don't have to rehash the past. I just want to be there for you now and I want you to know that I never stopped loving you," Cassandra assured him. Will didn't know what to say because she became the bigger person and he felt so small at that moment. However, he was glad she called and offered her support. "I'm just happy to hear from you. I'm sorry about everything. I really messed things up with you. Now I know you were looking out for me," Will said, apologetically. "Like I said, let's leave the past in the past. I don't have any expectations. I just wanna be there for you in your darkest hour," Cassandra told him.

Will was ecstatic. He thought he had lost Cassandra forever after the stunts he pulled, but in reality, he was just getting cold feet when Cassandra started to demand a commitment from him. Will was running to nowhere and his running got his ass into a whole lot of trouble. Being rich single and free has its perks, but being a millionaire athlete offsets all those perks. Will knew this was his second chance at love and he had better taken it. The fact that he could possibly go to jail for awhile without having a significant other in his corner, dominated his thoughts. As eager as he was to get things back to normal with Cassandra, she wanted to be there just to support him. She couldn't be any clearer when she told him, "Though I miss you, I'm not ready to jump back into a relationship with you right now, because you need to focus on your legal issues, and to make sure you walk away from this with your career intact." That was fair enough. Will couldn't ask for anything more.

Over the next few weeks, Cassandra and Will started to spend time together again, but there was no sexual interaction. They watched movies together and had dinner whenever possible at home, but that was the extent of it. She was also there to raise his spirit and offered herself as a character witness to his defense lawyer in case he needed it. Since Will had everything that the world had to offer at his home, there was no need to feed into the media frenzy by leaving his house. His home was outfitted with a bowling alley, movie theater big enough for twenty people, basketball and tennis courts, swimming pool and a chef on call whenever he craved a particular type of food. Being isolated from the public was not that big a deal. Cassandra was also fine with that. She wanted to protect him at all cost.

Will's parents and sister no longer had to worry about the possibility of him suffering from depression, because Cassandra was back in his life to make sure he stayed upbeat and ready for his trial in the upcoming months. They had peace of mind, knowing she was there. Will found the strength to return to his workout regimen in his home gym and kept his mind clear of the possibilities that lied ahead for him.

Chapter 15

Will also wanted to get to the bottom of his situation quicker than later. He wanted to hire a private investigator to check into the background of Amy Geller, the woman who accused him of sexual assault, but he received the assistance of his cousin Ray Ray for free. Ray had been watching the news and saw that Will was in serious trouble. As an FBI agent, Ray Ray had access to more information than the regular NYPD cops and any investigator Will could've hired. However, Ray Ray had no jurisdiction over the case. Having been an agent for so long, Ray Ray could smell a scam a mile away, but he could only supply information to Will's lawyer to prepare a good defense on his behalf. Ray Ray was more than happy to assist the lawyer on behalf of his cousin. Like most athletes who are completely oblivious to their status as bait or prey for gold-digging women, Will didn't go under the layers to see what could possibly go wrong with the outing with his friends and the strange women that night.

It didn't take long for Ray Ray to find the name Amy Geller on the FBI database. Of course, she had an arrest record for prostitution that was dropped a few years back, and many other miscellaneous charges for other minor infractions. To put it bluntly, Amy had a record. Though no felonies were found on her record, she had one nonetheless. Now it was up to Ray Ray to put all the pieces to the puzzle together. Because Ray Ray was working off the record, he couldn't focus solely on the case. However, he called Will to tell him that he was almost certain that he would be exonerated of all charges, because he could smell a scam brewing. Will was happy to know that there was some light at the end of the tunnel, but everything had to be done expeditiously in order for him to restore his good name and regain his job with the Falcons. Ray Ray's phone call to Will brightened his day and for the first time since the incident hit the news, he had a smile on his face that Cassandra noticed was very different since the day she had gotten back in his life. Will was back to his old sweet self again. The last words Will said to Ray Ray before hanging up the phone were, "I'm gonna owe you big time for this, cuz, I love you, man." To which Ray Ray replied, "That's what family is for. I love you too, bro." The two hadn't talked in a while, but there was an instant reconnection once they got on the phone.

Connecting the dots wasn't even as arduous a task as Ray Ray anticipated. Days after bringing forward her allegations, Amy's lawyer reached out to Will's lawyer to ask for a settlement to make the case disappear. Considering the fact that most entertainers, athletes or stars, usually settle quickly to make a case go away, even when they have been preyed upon, Will's lawyer felt he had to at the very least entertain the idea of settling with this woman just to make her go away. Not only did Will's lawyer undermine the fact that his client was innocent by entertaining this settlement agreement, he wasn't willing to fight for Will's integrity. He wanted to make the case go away as fast as possible, so he could move on to the next celebrity client. Having had a license to practice law in New York State, Cassandra suggested that Will fire his lawyer and hire her friend from law school who was also a practicing attorney in New York State. Cassandra offered her personal services free of charge to Will to help assist the attorney in New York. Contrary to popular belief, lawyers get paid whether a settlement is reached or if they have to go to court. That lawyer had reached his final days in Will's camp and it was time for a new strategy. Though Cassandra worked as corporate lawyer, she was more than willing to work her first criminal case on behalf of Will. She also made a call to her friend who was one of the best criminal defense attorneys in New York City. She had an impeccable reputation as a lawyer and Cassandra trusted she would do a great job representing Will. The two women were good friends in law school.

After the termination of Will's lawyer, Cassandra flew to New York City with Will to ask the court for a delay on the case, so she could prepare his defense. Luckily, the court agreed and she was granted a new court date in June. This time around, Will didn't have to question whether his lawyer had his best interest at heart, because her heart belonged to him and his to her. The two had begun to rekindle their relationship and Will was making plans to make Cassandra a permanent part of his life.

It was a good thing that Ray Ray hadn't reached out to Will's lawyer with more details, other than the fact that the accuser had a few misdemeanors on her record. After learning in the media that Will had fired his lawyer, Ray Ray called to make sure that the right person was hired this time. After Will told him that Cassandra was his new lawyer, Ray Ray was exhilarated. He had met Cassandra at

Tina's wedding and thought she was a good match for Will. He was impressed by her assertiveness and demeanor. Cassandra was the foundation Will needed in his life and it took this dire circumstance to make him realize that.

Chapter 16

Things were starting to get back to normal as Cassandra became the stabilizing force in Will's life. The court date was fast approaching and Cassandra was working diligently on a great defense for Will. She had even taken a six-month leave of absence from her job to dedicate herself to Will's case. Her focus was more research than anything, as her background in corporate law required her to offer research support on past cases. Will's case wasn't the first case heard in the media. There had been plenty of athletes accused of sexual assault crimes because a woman felt slighted by them. One of such cases was Mike Tyson's. While Mike may have been taken advantage of because of his celebrity status, his reputation as a monster in the ring preceded him in the courtroom. The prejudice used to convict Mike Tyson of rape was an abomination of the law. Had Mike walked this woman back to her dorm and allow her to be seen on campus with him, this case would have never been, Cassandra thought. Often times, athletes are too caught up in their glory and status, and it almost always becomes their downfall, something Cassandra, thought about. Cassandra didn't want Will to fall victim to the traps. Will had never gotten into any trouble or broken any laws in the past, but his reputation as a feared man on the field couldn't be erased from the minds of potential jurors. The brutal sport of football made Will, and it could possibly ruin him as well, but not under Cassandra's watch. Will meant too much to her for her to allow that to happen to him.

Meanwhile, Ray Ray had been in contact with her, keeping her abreast of everything and all the defaming information he found on Amy. Though Cassandra wanted transparency between her and Will during the course of her preparation for the case; however, she kept some vital information from him, because she didn't want to get his hopes up too much. Like the last lawyer she fired, Cassandra also received a phone call from Amy Geller's lawyer seeking a settlement. The number looked strange enough to Cassandra when she received the call, but she knew it was a New York number out of Manhattan. She picked up the phone on the second ring. "May I speak to Cassandra Russell?" the voice is heard through the receiver. "This is Cassandra. How may I help you?" she asked. "How ya doing, counsel? I'm reaching out to see if we can avoid the circus surrounding this case. My name is John Leibowitz and I'm counsel for Amy Geller. I'm sure you're aware that my client has a seal-tight case against your client, and we also have witnesses to corroborate her story. We can do ourselves a favor and save some embarrassment by settling this case amicably, and I promise all the charges will disappear. The state can't prosecute a case without a witness," Leibowitz said with confidence. Cassandra said nothing, while Leibowitz rambled on. "Ms. Russell, are you there?" he asked with hesitation. "Are you done?" she asked. "I'm done Ms. Russell," he responded. "I'll see you in court. Goodbye!" She hung up the phone on him. She didn't want to alert him to any facts that she may have found about his client. She wanted to present all her facts in court.

Cassandra had her suspicions that a scam was brewing and she was just waiting for Ray Ray to confirm her speculation. As it turned out, the group of women that Will met at the club, all knew each other. It wasn't by happenstance that they made their way to the VIP section where Will and his friends were roped off. Will and his entourage were preyed upon and they had no idea who was behind the whole thing. Like a good detective, Ray Ray worked tirelessly to put the pieces together. The scam he discovered was not all that original, but most athletes had fallen victim to it in the past, and Will was lucky to have Ray Ray in his corner. The stage was set for the showdown and Cassandra was about to go the distance to prove her man's innocence in court.

Chapter 17

As the stress on Tina's mind abated, she became her old jovial self again. Her relationship with Abigail was also being taken to new heights. Tina and Abigail now talked on the phone regularly like regular girlfriends do. They went shopping together, out to eat and even planned to go to Miami together on a girls' trip. Darren saw nothing wrong with his wife and assistant becoming closer friends. It actually took a load off him, because he didn't have to entertain his wife as much anymore. Tina also didn't bother Darren as much for sex anymore. She finally was able to keep herself occupied enough to the point where she didn't even bother for sex anymore. Darren was a happy man. He became more efficient at work and acquired more clients than he ever dreamed of. Business was booming!

While business may have been booming for Darren, he wasn't spending much time with Tina. His workload almost doubled and he spent more and more time at the office. He was consumed by his work. Though Tina didn't complain, she felt a little neglected by her husband, but she didn't want to come off as needy. While Darren cared more about meeting deadlines, Tina wanted to live life, and just like a woman, shopping became the cure for her neglect. Tina became a shopaholic only because Darren wasn't spending much time with her. Even though Darren forced Abigail to work overtime occasionally, she stood up whenever she felt he was taking advantage of her. She also wanted to spend time with her new best friend and buddy,

Tina. Abigail was a loyal worker and did everything she could to make sure Darren's business was operating smoothly, but she didn't want to be consumed by her job like he was. Darren was very kind and generous by offering her bonuses whenever one was warranted. Abigail was also a woman who enjoyed shopping and eating out, so she would join Tina on her shopping sprees and Tina was generous to her as well. Tina was now affectionately referring to her as Abby. She got whatever she wanted when she and Tina went shopping. Darren was making so much money and spending so much time at work, his guilt prevented him from setting any kind of limit on Tina's new spending habits. As long as the bills were paid and there was enough money in the savings accounts, everything was fine.

The more time Tina spent with Abby, the closer they became. When Darren would go to the office on a Saturday instead of spending time with his wife, Abby would step in to fill the void. They were like a family. Often times, the two women would get hounded by men everywhere they went. However, Abby was the alpha female who always put these men in their place. She was very protective of Tina. Abby was even shocked when Tina decided to take her to her parents' house with her one day and introduced her as her new best friend. She was like the sister Tina never had and Tina's mom started treating her as such. Her dad didn't feel the same way about Abby, though. One day he decided to question his daughter about her behavior as a married woman when she visited him at home with Abby in tow. "Tina, you have to remember that you're a married woman.

You can't be running around with this woman, who's obviously single. That'll lead to trouble. You need to focus on your husband," he said to her. Tina was taken aback by her father's comments, because he had never meddled in her business before. It took a few minutes for her father's words to set in, but Tina felt the need to let him know why she was running around with Abby. "Daddy, I know you think Darren is the perfect guy and he can do no wrong as long as he takes good care of me, but my marriage is like any other marriage. It's not perfect and Darren is not the perfect husband. I love him, but he spends most of his time at work now and leaves me home to be by my lonesome. So I made a friend, what's wrong with that?" she said. Mr. Allen, Tina's father, took a long deep breath before addressing his daughter, "That's what's wrong with the new generation. You have no patience and you expect your relationship to be perfect without putting any work into it. That man is working hard to establish his business and it may take him away from you for a little while, but he's doing all that because he loves you and wants you to have the kind of life that you're accustomed to. It doesn't mean you should be running around in the streets with your friend. That's how problems come about. When I first started my company, your mother and I barely spent time together, because I was always at work making sure my company was successful. That took a while, but eventually I slowed down, and your mother was home waiting for me every night. How do you think this man feels about you running the streets all the time?" Though it may have sounded like an attack, Tina didn't take it as such. She understood her father's old school teachings, but she also wanted to live her life her own way.

Mr. Allen got his words off his chest and never received a response from his daughter. Tina didn't want to be disrespectful at his house, so she kept silent. Before the conversation could escalate to something she didn't want, Tina walked back to the living room to get Abby and told her to gather her things because she was ready to leave. She hugged her mom before quickly walking out the door to head straight to the mall with a frown on her face, as if her father's words had hit home.

The following weekend, Tina and Abigail flew to Miami for some much needed fun in the sun. The two of them had a ball in South Beach. They went out to dinner at some of the nicest restaurants in South Beach. They visited the nightclubs, the bars, and partied their asses off. Tina also went shopping and brought a few items back for her husband. Of course, Darren missed her body next to him at night, but he knew she was coming back soon enough.

Chapter 18

Darren had one of his worse days since he opened his business. He couldn't wait to get home and free his cluttered mind of his daily worries. He looked like a defeated man when he walked through the door with his tie loosened; half of his shirt hanging out of his pants, and his looks completely disheveled. That would soon change when he set foot inside his house. Tina was standing at the door ready to wait on her husband hand and foot. From the sound of his voice earlier during a phone call, she sensed her husband wasn't having one of his best days. Darren had accidentally deleted the file of one of his clients, and he had to start all over again, which was a lot of work. The idea of going through all the receipts and the paperwork submitted by this client was tedious enough, but it was a client that Darren couldn't afford to lose. He needed to do whatever needed to be done to keep that client.

Darren struggled to open the door, while carrying his briefcase and the other folders with the client's paperwork. He dropped the folders and papers flew everywhere. He got on his knees and tried to gather the pieces of paper from the floor. Finally, after twisting the doorknob, he raised his head and was pleasantly surprised by what was standing before him. He never anticipated what he found when he set foot inside the house. The site of Tina in a nice robe with a bottle of massage oil in her hands and the urge to take away Darren's stress changed his demeanor instantly. "I don't want you to say anything. I just want to take care of my man today," Tina told him. She grabbed his hand and led him to the living room where she had a massage table waiting. Tina stopped by the store and purchased the portable massage table on her way home from work. She also stopped at the local aromatherapy store to get her favorite scented candles. She left work early enough to cook dinner, set up the massage table, ran a nice bubble bath in the Jacuzzi tub for her husband, and filled the house with lighted scented candles. All the lights throughout the house were turned off. Tina created a pathway to the bathroom with lighted candles and Rose petals. The aroma was perfect and the soothing atmosphere was even better. Darren had no choice but to relax.

After that long talk with her dad, Tina reflected on what her father was saying to her, and realized that she hadn't been catering to her husband enough, lately. Though Darren didn't complain to her, she knew she hadn't been tending to his needs. This man needed some tender loving care and Tina was about to bring it. Darren's demeanor changed almost instantly at the idea of being pampered. He didn't want to know what prompted this, and nor did he care. He just wanted to enjoy the moment.

First, Tina needed to get Darren completely naked. The sensual massage she had in mind could only be implemented on his bare skin. Darren didn't fight her attempts to pull off each clothing item, piece by piece, until he stood completely naked in the center of the room. She then grabbed his hand and led him to the table that was covered with a large soft towel. The atmosphere was so great Darren automatically began to relax his mind. A special kind of bonding was about to take place between Tina and Darren, something they had never done in the past. With the mood set and Darren now lying on the table, Tina couldn't wait to help release his tension. She placed a small bucket filled with hot water and a washcloth under the table to rid his body of the toxins. Tina asked Darren to lie on his stomach, while she cleansed his body with the wet washcloth. The soothing touch of her hands against his skin was relaxing. She slowly rubbed the wet washcloth against his skin as if to remove all of the stresses of the day. Darren was tickled when Tina began to clean his buttocks. She didn't only clean them; she carefully caressed them with her hands in an attempt to relax his muscle. As the hot water started to heat up his body, his pores were opening, giving way to the nice massage to follow. Darren turned on his back to allow Tina to wash him using the same routine and technique. He couldn't help getting aroused when Tina ran her hands down his chest with the hot washcloth. However, that wasn't the plan. Tina didn't want to have sex with Darren, at least, not yet, anyway.

After cleaning Darren's body from head to toe, Tina proceeded to turn on the stereo. She cued the Priceless Jazz Collection CD featuring Billie Holiday, Ella Fitzgerald, Louis Armstrong, John Hartman, Sonny Rollins and a few other jazz greats. At the sultry sound of Billie Holiday's voice while singing, 'Good Morning Heartache,' Tina began to rub her hands together, heating them up so they could be warm to the touch. She grabbed the warm massage oil bottle she kept wrapped in a heating pad, poured oil in her hands, rubbed them together and began the massage of a lifetime from Darren's toes. As she rubbed her way up, Darren felt complete bliss. She momentarily stopped between his inner and outer thighs to slowly caress them with her hands. By the time she got to his erogenous zone, Darren's twelve-inch penis was looking for some kind of attention. Though she dwelled on the erogenous zone, she never once touched Darren's penis. She began to knead his buttocks and the area right above it. That sensual pressure point drove Darren nuts. He had no idea his wife was so talented. The instructional video for massages that Tina bought was paying off, big time. Tina continued to massage the pelvic bone area. She also went from his calf to his back, creating energy with her hands that Darren had never experienced before. She used her hands in a sweeping motion around his chest area down to his stomach to draw energy towards his intimate zone. Darren's dick was hard as a rock and Tina was giggling inside, knowing how badly her husband wanted to make love to her.

After the massage was over, Darren got up with his hardened dick bouncing up and down, as Tina led him to the bathroom where a warm bath awaited him. The mood was continuous as Tina made her way upstairs with Darren in tow. By then, the CD had jumped to Duke Ellington's "The Jeep Is Jumpin'" and the stairway was lit with candles. As Darren set foot in the jetted tub, he let out a soft "Ahhhh." Tina's efforts were appreciated and she could see the disappearance of frustration had been replaced with relief. Darren slowly eased his way down into the tub, closing his eyes to the complete serenity of the situation. Tina freed herself from her robe and slid into the tub behind her husband with a sponge in her hand. She began to rub the soapy sponge sensually across her husband's chest with one hand, while massaging his pecks with the other hand. The moment was heavenly as Darren allowed himself to relax and just enjoyed the treat bestowed upon him by his wife.

The session was about to reach its climax in the tub. Tina moved from behind Darren and slid herself between his legs, with her back to his chest. Darren now began to massage his wife's breasts slowly, while pouring water from the sponge over her body. Tina's nipples were as erect as they could get, as the tingling feeling between her thighs started to emerge. She soon turned on her stomach to face Darren. She found his twelve-inch hardened dick sticking up out of the water. She slowly grabbed hold of it and started gently stroking it. Darren leaned back, closed his eyes and allowed Tina to take charge. The loud sigh from Darren only confirmed that he was enjoying his wife's hand around his dick. It didn't take long for Tina to wrap her lips around the shaft of his dick as she loosened her tongue around it. Tina had become somewhat of an expert at oral sex and Darren enjoyed every little improvement she displayed. "Oh yeah," he cooed, while the shaft of his dick rested in the warmth of her mouth. Tina went up and down and around with her tongue, soothing every inch of blood filled skin on his dick. She watched his facial expression as she encouragingly pleased him. The oral session went on for about fifteen minutes before Tina plopped her ass down on his hardened dick enjoying each inch as she made her way down to the base of his nuts. "Oh shit! That feels so good," she announced after finally taking all twelve inches inside her. Darren obliged her by softly stroking her with the water splashing around her ass. He held on to her tiny waist, as he slow-grinded his dick into her heavenly wall. It was intoxicating as the thrust of his dick into her vagina took him to new heights. Darren needed that, but Tina wanted it even more. She started massaging his balls as the speed of her movements increased. Tina was about to cum and it was going to be explosive. She let go of his balls to grab hold of his thighs for comfort. Her liberating stance while she rode his dick, only pushed him to the brink of climax. Darren wanted to cum inside his wife, while she came over him. His grip around her waist tightened and she knew she was fast approaching her destination. This was common place for her. She started to wind uncontrollably as her legs shook over him. She was cumming, more than once. She came once more again, he did too. She could feel his last stroke all the way up her back before he slightly loosened his hands from her waist. Mission accomplished.

   After Tina and Darren came out of the tub, they went downstairs to the dining room where Tina had dinner ready for the two of them. The time Tina spent much watching the cooking channel was paying off. Her meals tasted better every time she cooked, and her husband never complained about her cooking. Shrimp scampi was the dish of the night. They both ate heartily before washing it all down with a glass of red wine. The smile on Darren's face at the dinner table was all the appreciation Tina needed. "I know we've had appetizers upstairs, and we're having the main course right now, but I think I want dessert, too," said Darren. "When have I ever turned you down for dessert?" Tina asked in a naughty way. Darren smirked, because he knew exactly what he was going to do to his wife once they went back upstairs. Nothing needed to be said, it was the best night's sleep he had in a long while.

Chapter 19

As things fell back into normalcy at the office, Darren started to become increasingly uncomfortable with Abigail's subtle flirtation with him. The curiosity in her eyes was enough to keep him locked up in his office most of the day without face -to-face contact with her. Darren chose to engage with Abigail through the phone whenever things started to heat up a little more than they should. It wasn't just Abigail, but Darren was also developing a weakness for her beauty. This was something he needed to address, but had no idea how. Abigail didn't help matters much by showing up in the office looking as delicious as she wanted to be every day. She knew there was a fine line between proper and improper behavior, but she let her body language do all the talking. Darren was fighting temptation every day and he knew he couldn't fire Abigail. He had grown too dependent on her. He couldn't manage his business without her and the cost to hire someone new was too much to bear.

The commercial printer positioned right at the corner of the entrance of Darren's office was daily torture for him. Abigail somehow managed to make copies of her files only when Darren's office door was wide open and he was sitting at his desk. Like most beautiful women, Abigail knew her greatest physical assets would be Darren's weakness, and she tested him at every turn. The way she stood at the printer and caressed those keys as she entered the correct amount of copies to be printed for each page was grueling for Darren to watch. Her attire, though professional, was always sexy. The visual journey from her bare ankles all the way up to her thighs as she leaned over, while waiting for the copies to come out was unbearable. That visual alone was enough for Darren to consider masturbating. Sometimes he tried to block it out of his mind by telling himself he was in love with his wife, but that was only an exercise. Deep down, he knew he wanted to throw Abigail on his desk and pound her pussy until she came. However, crossing that line wasn't an option.

Darren needed to develop new coping mechanisms in order to keep from jeopardizing his professional relationship with Abigail. He was banking on Abigail's hook up with Will to stop all his desires to slip up and accidentally fuck her, but that didn't pan out. The two of them subconsciously accepted the daily flirtations going on, but each questioned in their minds if it would ever go beyond that. Pushing the limits was one thing, but violating Tina's trust was something completely different. Since Tina and Abigail were now close to best buds, she sometimes confided in Abigail about all things, including her husband. She was never shy about talking Darren's twelve-inch penis and how well he fucked her in the bedroom. In a way, maybe Tina was trying to open the door to something more, Abigail sometimes thought. Abigail even caught her own glimpse of Darren's twelve-inch snake one day.

She couldn't believe how delicious his dick looked and almost wanted to wrap her lips around his Mr. Goodbar to suck the chocolate off his dick once. This incident took place when Darren went to the bathroom and failed to lock the door behind him. It just so happened that he was envisioning his wife's mouth wrapped around his dick as a new coping mechanism to keep Abigail off his mind. His hand was covered with the thick white lotion that he poured from the container sitting on the bathroom sink. He might have stroked his dick once or twice, but he decided it would be inappropriate to masturbate at work, while his assistant was in the next room. As he was about to pull his hard dick pack into his pants, Abigail turned the knob and walked in without looking in front of her, while pulling up her skirt to go sit on the toilet. She never even saw him standing in front of her with his dick in his hand, at first. It was an awkward moment for both of them. Darren held his dick in his hand covered with a white substance that looked very close to semen, while Abigail had her skirt up and her panties half way down her thighs. If anything was going to happen, this would be the time. She was startled when he said, "What are you doing?" However, embarrassed because of their mishap, Darren quickly turned as Abigail dashed out of the bathroom, but not before she took a long look at his erect dick.

The conversation that followed wasn't the most comfortable, but they both attempted to explain their mistakes. "I'm very sorry about barging in on you like that. I almost peed on myself, so I was rushing to the bathroom and opened the door without knocking," Abigail explained. They both chuckled to lighten the moment. "Nah, it was my fault for not locking the door behind me. I promise that won't happen again," Darren said, while avoiding eye contact with Abigail. Darren's twelve-inch was in full view when Abigail barged into the bathroom, and he knew it. Though Darren was not at all a braggart, he knew that he was more blessed than most men. Now, he secretly wondered if Abigail sized him up or not. Abigail secretly wondered if the site of her shaven pussy could've been the reason why Darren's dick was so hard, however quick a glance he might've taken of it. At least she was able to confirm everything that Tina had said about her husband. She wasn't making any of it up. Darren, in fact, had a huge dick and it looked appetizing to her.

Chapter 20

Meanwhile, the defense was finally ready for Will's big day in court. There were countless people on the witness list for the prosecutor, but none would prove more damaging than Eddie Morganton, also known as Fast Eddie. Monday couldn't come quick enough. The morning was a little more brisk than usual in early June. The sun was out and the glare of the spring sun radiated against the trees and all the natural inhabitants of the Earth. Will had flown in that past Friday to start his weekend in New York. Though he and Cassandra had made a promise of abstinence during the course of his trial, it was sexual bliss when the two of them checked into this cozy hotel on Manhattan's east side together that weekend. The close quarters brought all the dormant emotions to the surface. What happened between them was inevitable. Perhaps the coziness of the room with the California king size bed and boutique-like décor brought out the beast in them.

While Will may have been craving Cassandra's touch, she was thirsting and yearning for his dick. It only took the meeting of their eyes after they plopped down on the king size bed for them to realize their promise of abstinence was soon going to be thrown out the window. The lust in Will's eyes moistened the depth of Cassandra's pussy. She hadn't seen that look in while, but she knew it was a familiar look of satisfaction she saw from Will in the past. He wanted to satisfy her. Will didn't even bother kissing her, before lifting her above his head, so she could wrap her legs around his neck. Her skirt rolled right above her thighs and her dripping panties were anticipating the attack of Will's tongue. Being a strong and powerful athlete worked to Will's advantage. Cassandra felt like Olive Oil on the shoulders of Popeye after he swallowed a can of spinach whole. Will slowly moved her panties to the side as his tongue crept into the depth of her pussy. Cassandra held on to Will's head for balance as her eyes rolled up and down in her head to the calming feeling of Will's tongue against her clit. His mouth was covered with her juices. Cassandra's head was above the clouds from oral euphoria. "Lick me, baby," she uttered. Will wasted no time resting the tip of his tongue on the tip of her clit and rolled it up and down like a paintbrush to get her to scream out a nut. "I'm cumming! Baby, I'm cumming. Oh God I'm cumming!" she exclaimed.

The big teddy bear was just getting started. For a big guy, Will didn't pack much more than eight inches, which was perfect for Cassandra. The last guy she dated with a bigger dick almost tore up her cervix. Will gently placed Cassandra on the bed on her stomach. She arched her ass up and spread her legs, leaving nothing to Will's imagination. The pinkness of her beautifully carved pussy was adrenaline to Will's dick. He wet his fingers in his mouth before inserting the index in Cassandra's pussy. Will finger-fucked Cassandra with one hand as he smacked her ass with the other. Cassandra wasn't your average woman, she was a freak, and so was Will. The moaning and groaning increased at the movement of Will's finger, but Cassandra almost lost it when Will stuck his tongue in her ass. That was her pleasure zone and Will could make her cum at will whenever he licked her ass. Will was munching on her ass like it was the Hostess Company going out of business. Cassandra held on tight to the sheet as Will inflicted pleasure on her. "Oh baby, I miss that tongue. Lick my ass!" she exclaimed. Will was deep in her ass with his tongue while his index finger searched for her G-spot. Cassandra couldn't keep still as she was in search of an explosive nut. Will knew he hit her spot when her thighs started gyrating, and her pussy squirted a clear liquid all over the bed. Cassandra only squirted when her orgasms were magnified, but Will knew she was due for one.

Will had a satisfying look on his face as Cassandra's tired body lay still on the bed. Her eyes were glazed and sweat beads formed all over her forehead. She also took short spurts of breaths as she stared at the man who just rocked her world. "I got you next round," she said to Will, while taking a break. "It's ok, babe. You know how much I enjoy satisfying you. It's all about you right now." He comforted her. The conservative look that Cassandra sported in the courtroom was completely opposite of who she was in the bedroom. And Will just loved that about her. 'A lady in the street and a freak in the sheets,' was the mantra by which she lived. Nobody could guess that Cassandra was so freaky. When they first met, Will actually thought Cassandra was a virgin. Unbeknownst to him at the time, she was to become the best sexual partner he had ever met.

After a quick rest, Cassandra rolled over to find Will's eight-inch dick standing hard enough to serve as a beam holding up the foundation of a house. Though not overly long, Will's dick was very thick. It was always a mouthful for Cassandra. Will was laying on his back with his eyes fixated to the ceiling as if he was deep in thought. However, he was soon shaken out of his trance when Cassandra wrapped her lips around the head of fat dick. Her soothing tongue brought warmth and comfort and Will welcomed every minute of it. "Yes, baby," he cooed as she maneuvered her tongue in a circular motion around his dick. Will wasn't the only one in the relationship who knew how to drive his partner crazy. Cassandra also had a couple of tricks of her own. She spat a little saliva in her hand to get it nice and slippery before commencing to stroke Will's dick from the base, near his nuts, all the up to the shaft and ending it with her tongue on the head. The combination of her tongue and hand stroking his dick resulted in a brewing nut inside Cassandra's mouth. Will couldn't help grabbing the back of her head and holding on to it while he let out a shot of warm semen down her throat. Cassandra swallowed his seed without flinching.

After a brief recuperating period, Will's dick was standing rock hard again and searching for the perfect compartment to fit in. Cassandra welcomed him with open legs. She lay on her back on the edge of the bed as Will stood in a squatting position to penetrate her, while holding her legs up. Will got his kicks out of watching his dick slide in and out of Cassandra's pussy. The nightlight provided just enough illumination for Will to allow himself to be a spectator to his actions. His strokes were nice and slow. He couldn't help pulling the skin back that hung over

Cassandra's oversized clit, so he could rub it with his finger. He licked his thumb before placing it on Cassandra's clit in a circular motion as he stroked her. He felt heavenly to her. Her slow moans gave him encouragement. He rubbed her clit a little harder. She rested her left leg over his shoulder and the other leg stood suspended in the air. Will's thick dick filled her pussy completely, but she also wanted his deep strokes. He pulled her towards him as he tried to reach the bottom of her pit. "Mmmh!" she mumbled. "You like it deep, babe?" he asked. She looked up at him and said, "You know I do. Give it to me deep, baby." Will's slow strokes started to pick up steam like an old train. Her left legs now stood straight up against his chest as he stroked her hard. His body was so close to her, not even a sheet of paper could get between them. Cassandra was now yelling and begging, "Fuck me! Fuck me, babe! Harder!" Will obliged. His crotch and hers made clapping sounds as they met for each stroke. Will was covered in sweat, and Cassandra's hair was all over the place. It was time to switch position.

Will bent her over the bed and spread her legs open to penetrate her from behind. Cassandra's ass never looked any better. Because of his big frame, Will had to spread his legs apart very wide in order to meet the height of Cassandra's pussy. His athletic training came into play as he needed to balance himself, while stroking Cassandra from behind. The sting of his hands against Cassandra's juicy ass only excited her more. "Smack my ass!" she yelled at him as he fucked her. "Yes, baby. Fuck me hard and smack my ass," she kept saying. Will was almost out of breath as he simultaneously smacked her ass and stroked her. "Here it comes, baby," he announced as his nut neared. "I wanna cum with you," she told him. She started winding harder and faster against his dick. "I'm cumming too, baby," she announced. He grabbed two hands full of ass as he came hard inside her pussy. The two of them came almost at the same time.

They both crashed on the bed and ended up spending most of the weekend in their hotel room. Since the media was hunting for Will, Cassandra thought it was best if he stayed out of sight. They fucked each other's brains so much that weekend they were spent by Monday morning. However, Cassandra was more than prepared to present her case to the judge and jury.

Chapter 21

Cassandra dressed to kill that Monday morning for court. She wore a power business suit with dark blue pants suit, a baby blue collared shirt and a nice pair of black three-inch heel shoes. She also made sure Will dressed appropriately for the mostly white jury that he had to face during this trial. Will wore a tailored navy blue single-breasted suit, and a gray striped shirt and a solid grey tie with black shoes. They looked like a power couple as the livery black Lincoln Town car picked them up from the hotel. They looked more like a couple than client and attorney. Cassandra carried her briefcase and another bag over her shoulder filled with papers that she would need for the case. The two of them were at ease and relaxed on the ride to the courthouse. Cassandra reached out to grab Will's hand to comfort him. He held on to her hand tightly like a baby trying to keep his mother from walking away. By the time they got to the courthouse, the chaos had already begun. Scores of reporters aligned the steps and cameras were flashing from every direction as they tried to get a statement from Will. Cassandra and Will pushed through the crowd to find their way into the halls of the courthouse. When they opened the door to the courtroom, Will's parents, Tina and Darren were all sitting in the front row for support. It was solidarity in its highest form.

The judge hadn't yet entered the court room, so the family got a chance to chat with Will and told him they loved and supported him in every way. Will was relieved that his entire family was there for support. The family was looking for relief and they couldn't wait for the proceedings to start. After about fifteen minutes of chatter, the court officer announced the Judge and asked that everybody stood up. After Judge Bernstein took his seat, he asked the prosecutor and defense if they were ready to present their case. The prosecutor announced he was ready. The defense also said they were ready. Cassandra and Chandra knew there would be holes all over the prosecutor's story and the dots were not going to connect, so they took out their pens and pads to take note. This was a case the prosecutor wasn't willing to lose, but there's always a first time for everything, and Cassandra and Chandra wanted this case to be his first loss.

The young prosecutor, Mr. Langley, wanted to win at all cost and so he began, "May it please the court, counsel, ladies and gentlemen of the jury, June 17, 2011 was a beautiful night in the city. It was a night that transcended what New York City life is all about. It was still late Spring and Ms. Geller woke up that morning looking forward to hanging out with some of her best friends. Ms. Amy Geller and her friends wanted to go out and enjoy all that New York has to offer; at least that's how she felt when she left her house. She took a shower, put on her makeup and wore one of her sexiest outfits, because she wanted to feel sexy, not to accost any man. Ms. Geller was feeling good about herself and she wanted to celebrate. However, all that would change when she arrived at club Amnesia on the lower west side of Manhattan in Chelsea. Ms. Geller and her friends were spotted by Mr. Stevens and his entourage, and he instantly became amused by her. A beautiful white girl with flawless skin, long flowing hair, a killer body and a great smile, she's every African-American athlete's dream. We all know that most African-American athletes dream of having a white girl on their arm," before Mr. Langley could finish his statement, the judge intervened and said, "Mr. Langley, your last statement will be stricken from the record. I will not tolerate any racial innuendos in my courtroom." Mr. Langley had already achieved his goal of planting the seeds in the minds of the jurors that most African-American athletes want a white woman. "I'm sorry, your honor. Ladies and gentlemen of the jury, please disregard my last statement," Mr. Langley said with what appeared to be a smirk across his face. He continued, "Ms. Geller and her friends were naturally excited when they were noticed by a celebrity athlete, so they decided to take Mr. Stevens' offer to join him in the VIP section of the club. The two groups partied together most of the night. However, Mr. Stevens couldn't get enough of Ms. Geller. He decided to invite her back to his hotel suite with him and his crew to continue the party. As a matter of fact, Ms. Geller was all done partying. She was ready to go home and call it a night, but Mr. Stevens insisted." The jury was hanging on every word spewed by the prosecutor. Cassandra and Chandra were trying their best to read the jury's body languages.

Mr. Langley went on, "After enough convincing from Mr. Stevens, Ms. Geller and her friends reluctantly agreed to go to the hotel suite to party with Mr. Stevens and his posse. She didn't have any reason to fear him, because it was a group of people. Ms. Geller never imagined a professional athlete would force himself on her, but that's exactly what Mr. Stevens did when he isolated himself with Ms. Geller in one of the bedrooms in the suite, by telling her he wanted to talk to her in private. Ms. Geller may have been gullible for trusting Mr. Stevens, but she should not be blamed for becoming a victim of his aggression. In plain and simple English, Mr. Stevens assaulted Ms. Geller, and I will prove to the jury without a reasonable doubt that Mr. Stevens is a predator and he should be locked up with the savages of his kind." There was a racial overtone filled with anger in Mr. Langley's voice. He was trying to appeal to the possible racist side of the jurors. He wanted to paint Amy Geller as the white victim of a savage black man who felt some kind of entitlement because of his physical gift on the football field.

Mr. Langley hadn't reached the end of his statement yet, "Ladies and gentlemen, the judge has explained to you one of the counts against Mr. Stevens is sexual assault. That is a crime in which the offender, Mr. Stevens, subjected the victim, Ms. Geller, to sexual touching that was unwanted and offensive. And then there are two more counts of sexual battery and aggravated sexual assault. Each of those counts has various elements. At the end of the case, the judge will instruct you on those elements. It is our burden to prove each of those elements for each count. Our job is to make your job easy by meeting that burden. We will present you with ample evidence to convince you beyond a reasonable doubt that Mr. Stevens committed these crimes. Mr. Stevens was sex crazed on the night of June 17, 2011 and he went after Ms. Geller and took his rage out on her. We're here to prove that celebrity status and money doesn't justify criminal behavior. Thank you, ladies and gentlemen, and thank you, your honor." Mr. Langley walked away feeling confident that he had painted a monstrous picture of Will Stevens and his case was all but won.

Now it was the defense's turn to present their opening statement, and Chandra couldn't wait to get started. Cassandra thought it would be best if Chandra presented the opening statement because she had been a practicing criminal defense attorney since obtaining her Jurist Doctorate from law school. The fact that she was emotionally disconnected from Will made for a better presentation, anyway. Cassandra feared her emotional attachment would supersede her efforts and would be detrimental to Will's defense. "May it please the court, your honor, counsel, ladies and gentlemen of the jury, this is going to be one of the toughest decisions that you'll ever have to make, because the very livelihood of this young man lies in your hands. I need to give you a little history about my client to prove to you without a reasonable doubt why my client did not assault Ms. Geller on the night of June 17, 2011. First of all, my client, Mr. William Stevens grew up in a loving home in Long Island with his lovely parents who are still married to this day." Chandra points to Mr. and Mrs. Stevens as she delivered her message. Will's mom and dad smiled at the jury. After engaging the jury with Will's parents, Chandra continued with her opening statement. "Mr. and Mrs. Stevens didn't just raise their children, but they also instilled values, respect and principles in them. Will was an all-state academic student athlete in high school who went on to become an all-conference academic student athlete in college. Will graduated with a degree in political science and aspires to become an attorney once his football career comes to an end. In addition, Will has set up a foundation to help shelter battered women in his residential state of Georgia, a month after he was signed to the Falcons. During his illustrious career as a linebacker in the National Football League, Will has never had any blemish on his record. He's not one of those athletes who go out of his way to seek attention. As a matter of fact, the defense will prove that it was Mr. Eddie Morganton, also known as Fast Eddie, who invited Ms. Geller and her friends into the VIP section where Mr. Stevens was seated." Chandra pointed to Eddie who was seated in the third row from the front in the courtroom. The jury turned to see a bewildered looking Eddie.

As things started to get underway, the prosecutor wondered what angle the defense was going to take, but the element of surprise would soon baffle everyone. Cassandra had Ray Ray to thank, because he broke the case wide open. Though Eddie was in the courtroom as a witness for the prosecutor, he would be the one to cause the greatest damage against the prosecutor's case. Everyone in the courtroom would find out the real motive behind Amy Geller's claim soon enough, should the case continue.

Chandra was just getting started. "Ladies and Gentlemen, you will also see and hear the evidence that will prove the sole purpose and the only goal of Ms. Geller is to extort money from Mr. Stevens. The defense will expose Ms. Geller and her cohorts as the extortionists that they are." After hearing Chandra drop the extortionist bomb, Mr. Langley had a confused look on his face. He had no idea where that came from. However, Chandra continued with her statement, "Finally, ladies and gentlemen of the jury, you will be provided with testimony from Ms. Geller herself that Mr. Stevens never once put his hands on her. Now, we have three counts of aggravated assault and sexual assault against Mr. Stevens that really are three cases in one. At the close of this case, Ladies and gentlemen, I will return. I will stand before you with the evidence and I'm going to ask you to base your verdict on the evidence presented for this case, and I'm going to ask you to return a verdict of not guilty on each of these counts. I believe at the end of this case, I will show that my client never had any malicious intent towards Ms. Geller. He never intended to have sex with her and he became a victim of Ms. Geller's greed and a quick money scheme. Thank you, ladies and gentlemen."

Chapter 22

The case was all set to move forward. The judge looked over to the prosecution's desk and then the defense's desk and asked, "Are both parties ready to move forward with the case today?" Both the defense and prosecution answered, "Yes." The judge looked towards the prosecutor and said, "You may call your first witness." After rummaging through his paperwork for a few seconds, Mr. Langley called Ms. Geller to the stand. The court officer placed her hand on the Holy Bible to swear her in before she took her seat on the witness stand. "Ms. Geller, can you tell the court a little bit about yourself?" Mr. Langley asked with a friendly smile across his face. It was apparent that he was trying to get the jury ready to listen to the story of the girl next door. "My name is Amy Geller. I'm twenty-eight years old. I'm originally from Minneapolis, Minnesota, but I've been living in the City for the last 10 years. I currently work as a waitress, while pursuing a career in acting." Amy started revealing the fabricated version of her "girl next door" story before she was abruptly interrupted by Mr. Langley with a wider smile across his face and said to her, "Tell us what brought you to New York City, Ms. Geller." It almost seemed like the two of them had rehearsed the performance they were displaying. "Well, I came to New York to pursue my dream as an actress. I've wanted to be an actress since I was a little girl. In high school, I was a member of the Drama and Shakespearean club. New York

City offered the best of both worlds. I could either be on Broadway or pursue a career in film."

Mr. Langley was a little too caught up in his witness' performance. "So, you came to New York City to make your dreams a reality, like many of the stars before you who came from other places to make it big in New York." Mr. Langley made it a point not to ask Ms. Geller about her educational background, because she was a high school drop-out who left school in the 10th grade after running away from home. A secret he tried to keep from the defense, but Ray Ray left no stone unturned as he dug into her background. Mr. Langley wanted the jury to be under the belief that Ms. Geller had graduated from high school and soon after moved to the City. "How has the experience in New York City been for you so far, Ms. Geller?" Mr. Langley asked, still cheesing. "So far, I've been enjoying New York and I've been going on many auditions trying to land a major role in a movie or a play. I love New York," she said. She was giving a stellar performance and the jury was connecting with her struggling artist story. "Ms. Geller, up until you ran into Mr. Stevens, you had been having a wonderful experience in New York, hadn't you?" he asked. "Yes sir," she answered. "Ms. Geller, were you happy as a child? Will you tell the Court about your upbringing," Mr. Langley asked her. Amy Geller flashed her rehearsed smile and looked toward the jury to recollect those fond memories as a child. "I was a very happy child and had a wonderful upbringing. My parents raised me with values and taught me to respect all people regardless of race, gender or sexual orientation. I was taught that everyone deserves a fair chance in life. Minnesota's not like New York, so I spent most of my time playing outside in the backyard with my friends. My parents didn't have to worry about our neighbors, because in my community, everyone looked out for one another." It was as if Amy was painting a picture of herself running through a Lilly garden in her favorite white dress as a child. She was happy and the jury connected a little too much with her make-believe story. Mr. Langley felt he was scoring major points with the jury. Now it was time to recreate the gruesome scene of the sexual assault that took place that night, according to Amy Geller.

Mr. Langley paced back and forth in front of the witness stand, trying his best to segue from beautiful child memories to a heinous sexual assault crime. "Ms. Geller, can you point out your attacker to the court please?" Amy Geller timidly looked towards Will who was seated at the defense table and pointed to him. "Let the Court acknowledge that Ms. Geller is pointing at Mr. Stevens who's wearing the dark blue suit." Once Mr. Langley identified to the court who the "sexual predator" was, he needed to move on with the rest of the testimony from the victim. "Ms. Geller, I know this is going to be difficult for you, but we need to change course and take you back to that gruesome night when you were attacked by a monster. A monster sitting in the courtroom that you may very well fear at this very moment…" Before Mr. Langley could finish his statement, the defense got up and interjected, "I object to counsel referring to my client as a monster, your honor." Cassandra wasn't going to sit back and let Mr. Langley demonize her man. She nudged Chandra the very first time

Mr. Langley referred to Will as a monster, and Chandra got up real fast to voice her objection. "Objection sustained," said the Judge. "Mr. Langley, we are conducting a trial here. You will refrain from referring to the defendant as a monster. I'm not going to allow any prejudicial statements in my courtroom. You've been warned." The Judge made it clear to the prosecutor he wasn't going to allow him to bend the rules in his courtroom. "I'm sorry, your Honor," Mr. Langley quickly said. However, he had already planted the seed of a monster in the minds of the jurors, once again. Mr. Langley was slick, but Chandra would prove to be more effective with her style later during the trial.

Mr. Langley refocused and asked, "Ms. Geller, how long did you know the defendant, Mr. Stevens?" He was trying to establish whether a relationship had developed between the defendant and Ms. Geller. Amy Geller suddenly became timid, while answering the question. She was trying to use her innocence to convey her message to the jury, as obviously rehearsed. "I had only met him the night of the incident when we were at the club," she answered. "Did you know he was a professional athlete?" asked Mr. Langley. "I had no idea who he was. To me, he was just a big guy who wanted to party with us at the club," she answered in a shy tone. "Why did you agree to go back to the hotel with the defendant, Ms. Geller?" Mr. Langley asked with a paternal tone. The shyness suddenly resurfaced. "We got to talking a little bit while we were at the club and he seemed like a nice enough guy to us, so we agreed to go with him because it was a group of us. I wasn't alone," she confirmed. "When you say we, what do you mean by that Ms. Geller?" Mr. Langley asked for clarity. "I meant me and my friends," she answered. "What happened after you and your friends agreed to go back to the hotel with Mr. Stevens and his posse?" Mr. Langley asked. However, Chandra quickly got up to object to his reference of a posse as it related to Will's friends. "Your honor, I object to the fact that counsel keeps referring to my client's friends as a posse or entourage. It creates prejudice in the minds of the jurors." The judge looked towards Mr. Langley and said, "Objection sustained." Mr. Langley wasn't winning the battle with the judge. His prejudices were right on the surface and the judge wasn't going to allow him to turn his courtroom into a circus. Mr. Langley had to change his strategy.

Feeling like he wasn't winning any favors with the judge, Mr. Langley decided to play nice enough to get his point across. "Ms. Geller, can you tell the court what happened after you and your friends agreed to leave the club with Mr. Stevens and his friends?" Mr. Langley asked with a bit of sarcasm emphasized on the word friends. "We all got in our cars and followed them to the hotel. When we got upstairs to the suite, there was a mini bar with liquor, a Bose stereo playing music from an iPod and Mr. Stevens called room service to order a couple more bottles of alcohol," she revealed. "So the mood was festive and you knew you were there for a party. Nothing's wrong with that. Ms. Geller, can you tell the court what happened a few minutes after the party began?" Mr. Langley was setting up the shot that would lead to the climax of the events for the jurors, and he wanted Amy Geller to deliver a blow by blow detailed account of what happened. "Well, while everyone was partying, I was dancing with Mr. Stevens. He was also trying to talk to me while we danced, but I couldn't hear him. That's when he suggested that we go into one of the bedrooms in the suite, away from the noise, so we could talk in private," she said, but Mr. Langley quickly jumped in to keep the story moving along. "What happened then, Ms. Geller?" he asked with anticipation. Amy Geller suddenly started trembling with fear, as if she was at an audition for a role in a scary movie. As fear gripped her, Amy Geller let out a soft sob before she began to tell the horrific story of that night. "I never thought he would turn out to be my worst nightmare. He was so gentle and kind at the club and when we were around other people, but it was like a metamorphosis transpired in the room. At first, he tried to grab and hold me tight in his arms, but I backed off. I didn't want to be that close to him. He pushed me into the corner by the bed where I had nowhere to go. That's when he grabbed me by the head and said, 'I want you to give me a blowjob.' I thought he was playing when I first heard it and then he said it again, in a forceful way. I was scared and didn't know what to do. I tried to get away from him, but he had his hands against the wall hovering around me. I told him I didn't want to do it, but he wouldn't listen. He pulled out his penis that was already hard and told me to put it in my mouth. He pushed my head down towards his crotch forcefully, and then said, 'If you bite it, I will smack the shit outta you.' I wanted to run out of the room, but he blocked my way. I'm only a hundred and fifteen pounds soaked and wet. I couldn't push him off me. I was afraid for my life, so

I opened my mouth and let him push his penis inside my mouth." Mr. Langley interjected again to create more compassion from the jury. "I know it's difficult for you to relive this horrific ordeal, but you need to let the court know the brutality you were dealing with that night and how your life was endangered by an aggressor who would not take no for an answer. I'm sorry you have to go through this, but you must tell your story." Mr. Langley played on the jury's gullibility.

By then, Amy Geller needed a box of tissue to wipe away her tears and to muffle her fake sobs. "I was kneeling before him as he pounded the back of my throat with his cock, I mean his penis. It went on for about fifteen minutes before he finally climaxed in my mouth," she tried to complete her story. "Where did he leave his semen, Ms. Geller?" Mr. Langley wanted to paint a nasty picture of Will for the court. Still sobbing, Amy Geller responded, "He held on to the back of my head and let it all down my throat because I didn't anticipate it. I started to gag and ran to the bathroom to try to spit out as much of it as possible." Cassandra had a different picture in her head. She saw a nasty white girl sucking her man's dick and taking down every drop of his semen down her throat, because she wanted it. She had that angry look on her face, but she remained calm as she took notes for cross-examination.

Needless to say, the graphic details put the jury in an uncomfortable position, especially the women. Chandra looked over to see the reaction of the female jurors, and she knew she had better pulled all the punches to save Will's butt. However, Mr. Langley was not done yet. He needed to ask Ms. Geller a few more questions before Chandra could cross-examine her. "Ms. Geller, what did you do after the incident?" he asked in a matter-of-fact way. Amy Geller was proud of her performance, now it was time to bring home the Oscar. "I ran out of the room and told my friends that we had to leave the party because I was scared," she said. Mr. Langley looked puzzled, as if he was trying to earn his own Oscar. "Did you go straight to the police, Ms. Geller?" he asked. Amy Geller now had her head down in shame as she answered, "I was too traumatized to go to the police. I went home and got in my bed, hoping to sleep away the nightmare that took place at the hotel." Though it seemed odd that she didn't go straight to the police to report the sexual assault, it is however, acceptable for sexual assault victims to delay reporting assaults to the authorities. "When did you report the assault to the police, Ms. Geller?" Mr. Langley asked sternly. Amy Geller looked almost embarrassed as she answered the question, "I reported the incident to the police the next day, after talking to my friends. I wanted to make sure that everything would be ok, given the fact that he's a celebrity and all." Mr. Langley was satisfied enough with her answer, but he had a few more questions. "Are any of your friends in the courtroom today, Ms. Geller?" he asked trying to justify the reason why she waited to report the crime. "No. None of my friends are here. They didn't want to get involved, because they don't want the paparazzi to intrude in their lives, which is the reason why I hesitated about reporting it in the first place. Ever since the case started, I have not had any privacy. I'm being followed all day by reporters and paparazzi everywhere I go," Amy Geller told the court, as if she regretted the decision to report the crime. "Ms. Geller, how do you feel about the defendant today?" This question was supposed to be the nail in the coffin. This is where Amy Geller would shine as a human being and paint a picture of Will as a sick man who needed help. "I'm afraid of him, but I don't have any ill will towards him. I think he needs to seek help for his sexual aggression, that's all," she answered. "Thank you, Ms. Geller. The prosecution rests at this time, your honor," Mr. Langley told the court before walking back to his desk.

Just as Amy Geller was trying to get up to make her way back to her seat, the judge stopped her in her tracks and told her, "Ms. Geller, you're not done yet." He then looked towards the defense table and asked, "Is the defense ready for cross-examination?" Chandra got up and asked that cross-examination continue after recess for lunch. The jury looked fatigued and Chandra and Cassandra needed to talk to Will to make sure they asked the right questions and totally destroy Amy Geller's credibility on the stand. "Court is adjourned for recess. I will see everybody back here in an hour," the judge announced before slamming down his gavel.

Chapter 23

Cassandra, Chandra and Will barely had any time to get something to eat. A Subway sandwich shop located down the street from the courthouse presented them with the best opportunity to munch on something. Will had a big appetite and he needed something in his stomach because he skipped breakfast that morning. The half dozen bananas he swallowed on his way to court vanished from his stomach and he needed a refill. The three of them sat at a table and ate meatball, chicken and chicken teriyaki subs. Will actually had one whole sub and the other halves of Cassandra and Chandra's subs. They washed their food down with bottled water before turning their attention back to the case.

Chandra made sure she took accurate notes based on Amy's testimony and what Will told her took place that night. The urgency to iron everything out with Will took precedence over conferring with Cassandra on the strategy to use for the case. "I've already seen way too many holes in her story. We're gonna have to tear her down. I need to make sure that you didn't miss any detail of what happened that night, Will," Chandra said to him. "I know that you said she sucked your dick on the bed, but were you at any time forcing yourself on her against the wall?" Cassandra asked with a little trepidation in her your voice. "I've already told you, this woman pulled me towards her and got right on her knees after we got in the room. She told me she wanted to give me the blowjob of my life. We never got a chance to move around in the room. Soon after I came in her mouth, we left the room. It was like she was on a mission," Will told them. Chandra shook her head and said, "As long as you keep your story consistent, we shouldn't have a problem. We have enough ammunition on this woman to discredit her story."

Cassandra and Chandra already knew that Amy Geller was no angel, but they needed to convince the mostly-white jury of her intentions. The sole black member of the jury was a woman in her sixties, and she seemed disgusted at the idea that a black man would forcibly sexually assault a white woman. She looked like she was right in the middle of the Civil Rights March with Dr. Martin Luther King, and facial expressions were pure disgust when she heard Amy Geller's tale of the events. It was like she couldn't believe how the young black folks of this new generation were failing the freedom fighters of yesteryears. However, Chandra wanted to appeal to her compassionate side. All they needed was one juror to vote "not guilty." Chandra's strategy was to show the injustice that was being conjured up against Will and how he was railroaded into the situation. After discussing it with Cassandra, they both agreed it would be the best strategy to use to secure a "not guilty" verdict. Still, their best weapon was the information that Ray Ray provided them with.

Returning to the courtroom, they hoped to discredit Amy Geller enough that the judge and the prosecutor would decide to drop the charges against Will, but that was a long shot, because most prosecutors don't like to throw in the towel. However, Chandra and Cassandra were ready to fight for Will all the way.

Chapter 24

It was about one o'clock when Chandra, Cassandra and Will made it back to the courtroom. Though lunch was supposed to last an hour, the judge didn't enter the courtroom until a half hour later. Meanwhile, the prosecution approached the defense with a deal that would send Will to prison for three years on a lesser charge. Mr. Langley was confident he was going to get a conviction, but Chandra was even cockier that her client would be exonerated of all charges. "I'm gonna make you look like the pompous ass that you are," Chandra said to Mr. Langley when after he approached her with the deal.

The judge entered the courtroom not a minute sooner after Chandra told Mr. Langley off. "All rise! The Honorable, Allen Bernstein, presiding," announced the Court Officer. Everyone stood up and then quickly took their seats after the Judge sat down. Chandra was certain that Amy had met with the D.A. to prep her for the cross-examination, but she was ready to tear her down. "Counsel, is your witness ready for cross-examination?" asked the Judge. Mr. Langley shook his head "yes." Amy Geller was brought back to the witness stand and raised her right hand on the good bible to swear under oath to tell the truth, the whole truth and nothing but the truth so help her God. Chandra glanced at her notes before approaching the witness stand to commence the tear-down of Amy Geller. "Good afternoon Ms. Geller. Please state your full name for the record." Chandra greeted her first, to make her feel at ease. "Good afternoon. My name is Amy Geller," she replied. "Ms. Geller, please adjust your microphone, so we can hear you clearly as you speak into it. Thank you," Chandra said trying to make the witness feel as comfortable as possible. Amy Geller arched her back and brought the microphone a few inches from her mouth. "Ms. Geller, can you please state your date of birth for the record?" Chandra asked. "June 3, 1983," Amy answered. "That makes you 28 years old today, correct?" Chandra asked, while looking at Amy Geller. "Yes," she answered. Chandra was just getting started. "Ms. Geller, on the night of June 11th, 2011, did Mr. Stevens approach you at any time at the club?" Chandra went straight for the gusto. She didn't want to beat around the bush. She hit Ms. Geller hard in her gut. "No. He didn't approach me…" Amy Geller was about to go on, but Chandra cut her off, "Ms. Geller, a simple no, sufficed. Thank you."

Chandra decided to take a step back before moving too fast. She knew she had enough damaging information on Amy Geller to bring this case to a complete halt in the courtroom. "Ms. Geller, what high school did you graduate from?" Chandra asked with her arms folded across her chest. "I attended Edison high school. Located on 22nd Avenue in Minneapolis," she answered. "Let me rephrase my question, your honor, because Ms. Geller didn't hear it correctly. "Ms. Geller, what high school did you graduate from, and what year did you graduate?" Chandra asked with her voice raised, so the jury can hear her. Amy Geller leaned forward and almost in a whisper answered, "I didn't graduate from high school." "We can't hear you, Ms.

Geller. Can you speak a little louder," Chandra asked. "I didn't graduate from high school," she said with an attitude. "Ms. Geller, can you tell the court in what grade you dropped out of high school?" Chandra calmly asked. "I left high school in the 10th grade," she responded. "What did you do after you dropped out of high school, Ms. Geller? The court be aware that Ms. Geller has used the aliases, Janet Burns and Nora Rogers in the past, but the defense will accept Amy Geller as her real name for now, your honor." Chandra surprised Amy. She was trying to counter Langley's strategy without getting on the Judge's nerves. "What did you do for work Ms. Geller, after you dropped out of high school?" Chandra asked with emphasis placed on work. "I worked as a prostitute, after I left home. My daddy was beating on me and my mother, so I ran away from home to be on the street," she burst out emotionally. The prosecution knew that Chandra was doing a good job breaking down the character of Amy Geller, so he quickly asked the judge if he could approach the bench.

Amy Geller had no idea what Chandra had in store for her. She thought she could waltz her behind into court and make Will look stupid because her white skin give her privilege. "Your honor, I didn't see this coming. Counsel never made any mention of a prostitution history. This shouldn't be admissible in this trial," the prosecutor argued. The judge was waiting for a rebuttal from Chandra. "Your honor, it is up to the prosecutor to ensure the due diligence of his witness. We're talking about ruining somebody's career here, your honor. This woman has more skeletons in her closet that a haunted house, your honor. She hasn't been honest about one thing, but if counsel persists, he'll find out this is just the tip of the iceberg. I recommend that he drops the charges against my client, or I'm gonna rip his witness to shreds," Chandra threatened. Mr. Langley was shaking in his boots, but he waited to hear what the judge had to say. "Mr. Langley, I'm afraid I'm gonna have to allow the questions, because they are related to the character of your witness. Just as much as you wanted to make her seem like an angel, you should've done your homework to make sure she wasn't the devil in disguise," the Judge told him. Langley looked toward his assistant sitting at the desk, and he saw a look of defeat on her face. "Ok, I'll agree to drop all charges against Mr. Stevens to put an end to this circus," Langley said. "Your honor, that's not enough. I want Ms. Geller and her conspirator, Mr. Eddie Morganton, also known as Fast Eddie, to be charged with extortion by the prosecution. They almost ruined my client's life and they're not gonna walk away scott free," Chandra warned. "And I want a public apology to my client from the District Attorney's office," Chandra demanded. "You're kind of pushing it, counselor. I'm dropping the charges against your client, shouldn't that be enough?" Mr. Langley said with a smirk on his face. "Mr. Langley, you're not doing me any favors. I have a complete file on your witness that shows she's been working as a call girl and Mr. Morganton is her pimp. I can go full blast to the media with this case, or you can just apologize to my client publicly? I also want the arrest expunged from my client's record," Chandra said with a definitive look on her face. "I believe what counsel is asking is fair, because Mr. Stevens stood to lose millions of dollars in endorsements and his good reputation as professional athlete," the Judge told Mr. Langley.

It goes without saying, but Will was ecstatic when he learned that his name would be cleared. He couldn't contain himself, so he planted a long kiss on Cassandra's lips. People in the courtroom had no idea that Will and Cassandra were an item, so they were a little perturbed by his reaction. Cassandra embraced him and welcomed his kiss. He was going back home a free man. The weight of the case was lifted off his shoulders. He didn't have to think about the possibility of prison or what he would do with the rest of his life. Will was free to think what the hell he wanted. The famous Dr. Martin Luther King quote was all that Will could think about. He silently said to himself, "Free at last, free at last, thank God, almighty, I'm free at last!" Now, he could plan his life with his future wife, Cassandra. She got away once, and he wasn't going to make the same mistake twice.

At the end of the day, Mr. Langley had no choice. He agreed to every demand Chandra made, and every demand was in writing. Both parties signed the agreement to help clear Will's good name. It took quite a few months for Will to repair his image and save his reputation. He hired one of the best public relations firm to help reconstruct his brand. Will gained back his reputation and many of the companies he endorsed came back with better contracts. The Falcons, however, apologized and Will forced a trade to the New York Giants, where he could be close to his family.

Chapter 25

Cousin Ray Ray was instrumental in the dismissal of the case against his cousin, Will. He worked tirelessly to find information on the "victim," Amy Geller. Through his investigation, Ray Ray learned that Amy was a teenage runaway who was in and out of juvenile detention centers in the Minneapolis area for prostitution. She decided to move to New York to get a new lease on life, but the trappings of the streets lured her right back in. While she was sincere in her aspirations to become an actress, Amy had no life-skills and needed to survive in New York. She went out to a club one night and met Eddie Morganton also known as Fast Eddie. She was amused by the handsomely rugged, former football star. Eddie's looks always superseded his athletic abilities, but coaches knew that women would come out to see him play. Though in his mind he thought he was good enough to one day become a professional athlete, everyone around him thought he was delusional. Eddie barely got enough playing time when he was in college. He decided to attend a division 1AA school, but even there he didn't excel on the field as much as he would've liked. He was limited athletically, but no one could tell him anything different. Eddie was Tim Tebow before Tim Tebow.

Eddie had a passion for the good life and wanted nothing more than to make a lot of money to live a life of luxury. While he may have thought his ticket to the good life was football, he was never dedicated enough to improve his skills on the field. Eddie was a ladies' man by nature. He stood 6ft-2inches tall and was ripped like a body builder from the time he was a senior in high school. His piercing blue eyes, smooth white skin and curly blonde hair made him a hit with the cheerleaders and all women his age that he came in contact with. While Eddie was a star with the ladies, Will was becoming one of the top prospects on the field. Eddie received local attention, while Will received national attention from some of the major colleges in the country. Will was recruited and offered scholarships by some of the major programs in the country, but Eddie never even got a first look. In order to play football, he had to walk on without a scholarship. Eddie, though, lied to his friends and family when he left for New Hampshire to go to college. Once on campus, Eddie did all he could to become the big man on campus. He hadn't even made the football team yet, but he was bragging about being the best tight end the school would ever see. Eddie, no doubt, looked like one of the most fit athletes on the surface, but he was not in football shape when he arrived on campus. During try-out, he was gasping for air after running the 40-yard dash. The coach wasn't too impressed with him, but he was good enough to add to the team without a guaranteed scholarship. Of course, Eddie parlayed his spot on the team as his star qualifier on campus. He wore his jersey almost every day to make sure everyone knew he was a member of the football team.

The first year of college went by relatively quiet for Eddie. He got into a couple of scuffles, but no major damage was done. He came close to getting his ass whipped at the end of his first year, but he backed down when he realized he couldn't win a fight against a much smaller guy with a much bigger heart than him. When Eddie returned to school his sophomore year, he vowed he was going to be a starter on the team. He tried as much as he could to develop better training habits, but he was too caught up with the ladies to stay focused. He was still a member of the team, but he saw very little playing time. One day the coach called Eddie's number only because the game was a blow-out and most of the scrubs were given a chance to prove what they could do. Running on a slanted route from the quarterback's play, Eddie took two steps and went down. He had to be carried off the field on a stretcher. Eddie blew his ACL and MCL ligament, an injury that was difficult to recover from. He left school after the injury and never returned.

Eddie always held some type of animosity towards Will since they were in high school, but he was too much of a chump to ever say anything to Will. Eddie was more of a pretty boy in a tough man's body. He also didn't work hard enough to earn the respect of the members of the football team in high school. The top-notch players, including Will, were hated by Eddie. His animosity would get worse after he dropped out of college. Now he was home every Saturday watching Will on television doing things on the field that he only dreamed of doing. Sports analysts were always bestowing praises upon Will for his hard work and dedication to the game of football and Eddie couldn't stand it. Once Will was pegged as a first round draft pick, Eddie almost lost his mind.

   The following year after Will was drafted by the
Miami Dolphins, he came home to find a jealous Eddie
trying everything to compete with him. The whole
community was now star-struck by the little boy who grew
up right before their eyes. Meanwhile, Eddie became a has-
been and got no attention from anybody. Will avoided Eddie
as much as he could that summer before leaving for training
camp. He knew Eddie was a hater and he didn't want to
jeopardize his career because of him. When Will came
home after his first season in the NFL, he bought himself a
Cadillac Escalade. That car raised the level of hatred in
Eddie to an all-time high. He couldn't stand the fact that
Will had made his dream a reality. Eddie could only think of
schemes to keep up with Will. He finally decided he would
use his best asset to obtain the lifestyle that he wanted.
Besides football, Eddie's other talent was his ability to win
over the ladies. That became his total focus.

   The night Eddie met Amy at this club in Manhattan,
he had already been a pimp for a few years and was earning
a lot of money with the five women who were working for
him. With the emergence of Myspace, Facebook and other
social networking sites, Eddie decided to take his pimping
game to the next level. He started an escort service where
potential clients had easy access to his bevy of women. He
was all about fulfilling their fantasy. Eddie was earning
thousands of dollars every day from his escort service, but a
pretty girl like Amy became a top earner for him. Having
been on the streets in the past, Amy already knew the tricks
of the trade, and she was more than willing to become an
escort. Eddie offered her better trappings than she had ever

seen. He offered her a nice apartment, a BMW and shopping sprees. Within months, Amy delivered like Eddie expected. She was his top moneymaker. Men were flocking to Amy and she drained them for everything they had. Eddie went from driving a BMW to a Bentley and Rolls Royce. Money was flowing his way like water, but Eddie couldn't get pass the idea of Will having a legit career, making legit money.

Will came home to see his family for a few days during the summer. He was driving around in his dad's car when Eddie spotted him at a red light. It was well-known information that Will was a multi-millionaire, but Eddie wanted to make sure Will knew he was balling, too. Eddie pulled up his convertible Bentley alongside Mr. Stevens' Cadillac CTS at the red light. He thought it was Mr. Stevens and he wanted to show off his new status. He was pleasantly surprised when he saw Will behind the wheel. This was his chance to show Will he had gotten even by becoming successful without football. He beeped the horn, and when Will turned his head, he saw a flashy Eddie wearing Dolce & Gabbana glasses and a velour-looking Versace sweat suit with the Versace logo plastered all over the suit, in the hot summer. "Will, what's up? It's Eddie," he screamed as he took off his glasses for Will to see. "Hey, Eddie, what's going on?" Will said. "Nothing, man, you know just trying to ball like you, bro," Eddie said, while pointing to his ride. "It looks like you're doing pretty well, baller," said Will. By then, the light changed and they needed to get a move on. "Pull over to the right, so I can holler at you for a minute," Eddie told him. Will pulled his father's car to the far right and jumped out to give Eddie dap. "Look at you, man. I see you tearing it up in Atlanta. You taking them boys to school," Eddie said in his best Hip Hop vernacular. Eddie always had a thing for Hip Hop culture, and he tried his best to emulate his favorite rappers. He even dressed like them, sometimes, but at the wrong time. Eddie and Will chatted for a few minutes and it was then that Eddie suggested he would get the rest of their friends together so they could hang out that night. It had been a while since Will had seen his boys, so it was no big deal to hang out with them. Eddie also lied to him and told him he owned a recording studio and a marketing company that did promotions for some of the major record labels in New York.

Chapter 26

Will was looking forward to finally hang out with his friends that he hadn't seen since he went away to college. He saw them in passing when he came home, but he never had the opportunity to hang out with them. Catching up with the fellas was what Will anticipated the most. He couldn't wait to find out what his friends had been up to and how life was treating them, but when he met Fast Eddie at the club in Manhattan, Fast Eddie was there with four flunkies that Will vaguely remembered back in high school. Fast Eddie was there to prove a point to Will that he was important and he had his own "yes men" that he controlled. Will wasn't even that type of guy, nor did he hang around people like that. Though Eddie made it obvious that his underlings took orders from him, Will treated the men with respect and dignity. He didn't want to make himself appear superior among his friends. The four guys actually were all fans of Will and they admired the fact that he made it all the way to the NFL. These four guys had fallen on hard time, due to drug addiction and lack of education, so Eddie used them for protection and to intimidate people in his line of work. All four of the dudes were pretty big and one of them was a known tough-guy since high school. They also played football, but they were not standout athletes. Will sort of knew who they were, but he acted like he remembered them well, to make them feel special.

Will was still game to hang out, even though it wasn't the people he expected. He could've made the decision to go back home, but he decided it would be wrong if he did that. While Eddie was trying a little too hard to make it known that the doorman and other bouncers at the club knew he was, Will simply fell back while the bouncers reached out to congratulate him. "Man, you're a beast on the field. I watch you play every Sunday," said the doorman with excitement in his voice when he saw Will. Suddenly, the spotlight was not on Eddie anymore and he couldn't deal with it. "I'm gonna make sure you get a nice table in VIP for the night. Give me a sec while I call one of my men to bring you in," said the head of security. Will, Eddie and the rest of the crew were ushered to the VIP section of the club. A couple of bottles of Greygoose, Ciroc with orange juice and cranberry juice were delivered to his table. The bouncers almost laughed when Eddie told them to put everything on his tab, like he had a tab at the club. Eddie was doing the most, while Will was in chill mode. A few women walked by to see who the big muscular guy sitting in the VIP was, but Will wasn't playing his NFL card that night. It was Eddie who decided to go into the crowd to grab the women that came to join them in the VIP section.

As it turned out, Eddie was looking to score major money from Will by extorting him. Through Ray Ray's investigation, he was able to discover Eddie's illegal dealings with his escort service and that information was passed on to Will's lawyers. However, he found out later that Eddie had planned to ruin his life that night, all along. When Amy Geller was charged with extortion, she decided to cop a plea and made a deal with the prosecutor for a lesser charge and less time in prison. Eddie was the mastermind behind the whole sexual assault case. He was hoping that Will would want to settle out of court with Amy to make his problems go away, but things didn't go according to plan. Amy told the DA that Eddie threatened to kill her if she didn't go through with it and he had planned to testify for the DA to say that he heard Amy screaming for help, while she was in the room with Will that night. Of course, the DA knew it would be Amy's word against Eddie's in a court of law, so he had her record a conversation with Eddie about the incident on her cell phone. Eddie threatened to put her in a body bag if she didn't keep her mouth shut, because the DA had no proof to charge them with anything. That conversation led to a fifteen-year prison sentence for Eddie and a one-year stint behind bars for Amy Geller.

Will thought Eddie had gotten over their differences since high school, but the animosity had only developed more because of Will's success. Tina was smart enough to recognize that Eddie never liked Will, and warned her brother not to be around Eddie, but Will wanted to give Eddie a second chance. It was also the last time someone ever got a chance from Will. He knew the only people he could trust were his family and love, Cassandra, who stood by him in his darkest hour.

Chapter 27

The entire family was happy and relieved that they were able to put Will's situation behind them. They had prepared for a lengthy trial, but fortunately, the case ended on the same day it started. That night, Mrs. Stevens and her husband decided to have a special dinner to celebrate their son. Everyone special to Will was invited to the shindig. Will's parents wanted to reaffirm their trust in their son. They never doubted the great job they did raising him, but they also wanted to make sure he understood that they would always be his support and loved him unconditionally. Mrs. Stevens would never admit it, but Will was her favorite child. She treated that boy like he was a prince when he was younger. It would've broken her heart if Will ended up in jail because of that incident. At night, she couldn't sleep and kept her husband up because she didn't know if her son would be able to handle prison. She had always been skeptical of the justice system as it related to black men, especially when the victim involved was a white woman. She knew that Will was guilty until proven innocent, but she prayed that God would protect her child. She undoubtedly loved her daughter, but her son was special to her. Mr. Stevens made it easy for his wife to play favorites, because he treated Tina like his little princess. She could do nothing wrong in daddy's eyes. However, he was a more stern with Will when it came to discipline.

Everyone arrived at the house in Long Island around six thirty that evening. Mrs. Stevens only cooked this much

Sexual Exploits Of A Nympho III   *Richard Jeanty*

food during the holidays, Christmas and Thanksgiving. That night they were giving thanks for a different reason. One of their children had been spared an injustice that many other young black men across America suffered every day. Will showed up with Cassandra on his arms, Tina came with her husband, and cousin Ray Ray came alone.   There were a few other family members there to celebrate with Will, mostly first cousins and distant members of the family. Mrs. Stevens called as many people who loved Will as possible. Will's generosity towards his family never went unnoticed. He never turned down a family member in need. At times, Tina had to step in when she felt certain members of the family were taking advantage of her brother's goodwill. He was glad to see so many people show up to the dinner to celebrate pretty much his freedom.

Everyone gathered in the living room and dining room to say a prayer before dinner started. Mr. and Mrs. Stevens instructed everyone to hold hands as they thanked God for saving their son from the devil's claws. Furthermore, they said a prayer for the wonderful meal that Mrs. Stevens cooked and for the opportunity to come together as a family. They took it to church in the house, that night.

Mrs. Stevens cooked everybody's favorite meals; macaroni and cheese, cornbread, black eyed peas, white rice, collard greens, honey ham, fried chicken, steak, pecan and sweet potato pie for dessert. It was a full house and everyone shared family stories when Will was a little boy. Ray Ray was known as the clown in the family, and he couldn't stop being a clown at the dinner. "Ladies and gentlemen," he announced to get everybody's attention. "I'm sure there's a guy in jail who's very happy because he's not gonna have to share his cell with Will. It doesn't matter whether I knew Will was a football player not, if I was in that cell, I knew I would be his bitch. Will's a big intimidating looking boy. Only a man about the size of Shaq would be able to turn Will to a bitch, and I already know my cousin don't even fly that away. You don't, right cuz?" he turned to ask to add a punch line to his joke. Everybody busted out laughing. Will just shook his head at his crazy cousin, because the boy ain't never changed, he thought. The mood was merry and everyone was having a good time.

No one knew or expected what was about to take place in the middle of Mrs. Stevens' living room. Will never gave any hint that he was going to do anything out of the ordinary, but he asked his big-mouth clown cousin to get everybody's attention for him, because he had an announcement to make. Naturally, it appeared as if Will was about to thank everyone for supporting him and for believing in his innocence, but instead, Will raised his voice and began to speak, "Ladies and gentleman, family, I am happy that we are gathered here tonight, because I have something special that I would like to do and I'm happy that my family is here with me while I do it." Will moved towards the middle of the room and got on one knee, while staring at his lovely girlfriend, Cassandra. He grabbed her by the hand, and pulled her towards him in the middle of the living room and said, "Cassandra, I want to take this opportunity to tell you that you are one of the best people I have ever met in my life. You're the most loving partner, my best friend and my happiness in life. I made the mistake of letting you go once, but I'm not about to repeat the same mistake twice. Like Beyonce says, 'I'm gonna put a ring on it.'" He pulled a three-carat oval diamond ring set in platinum out of his pocket, looked straight in Cassandra's eyes and told her, "Love is the only word that most of us know to describe our feelings for someone, but I only wish there was another word that people didn't abuse everyday just because. You mean so much to me and you make me so happy, love alone cannot describe how I feel for you. I adore you. I'm delighted by you. I treasure you. I cherish you. I value your love. I appreciate you, but most importantly, I love you with all my heart. Will you marry me?" Cassandra's face was draped with tears and the clinking of her teeth made the moment that much more unbelievable. Will poured his heart out to her like no man had ever done before. She was crazy about him and there was no other answer to give him but a big "Yes!" Cassandra jumped into Will's arms and kissed him like they were the only two people in the room. It was an unforgettable moment and Cassandra loved the fact that Will didn't hide his feelings and vulnerabilities even in the presence of his family.

After Cassandra accepted Will's proposal, everyone started clapping and the rest of the family moved in closer for hugs and to congratulate the couple. Will also asked his cousin Ray Ray to be his best man, and Ray Ray gracefully accepted. His clown ass also had one more joke left in him and there was no way he wasn't going to tell it. "Will, I almost wanted to marry you, too, bro. I'm gonna need you to write some of them words down for me, but just act like you've never heard them before if I ever tell them to a woman in your presence. I'll be looking out for your romance novels, too, bro. That's some book type shit you just dropped, bro." Everyone was laughing at his clown ass. It was a wonderful night and the family reconnected once more. The last time the whole family was together happened when Tina and Darren got married. Now, they had Will's wedding to look forward to.

Chapter 28

Tina could finally breathe easy. Her brother was no longer in the spotlight and things could finally get back to normal. She was the cornerstone for Will, beside Cassandra. The two have them have been close since childhood and she worried about her brother. Tina tried as much as she could to keep her brother's spirit up. She talked to him on the phone every single day and assured him that he was going to emerge victorious from his dilemma. She sometimes prayed with her brother over the phone and even shed tears for him whenever doubts kicked in. Now it was time for Tina to focus on her husband. Darren never complained to her about anything. He understood that her brother needed her, and simply stayed out of the way. Darren also buried himself in his work in order to keep his mind occupied. The long hours at the office also meant that he had to spend more time around Abigail. Though sympathetic, Abigail felt there was a void in Darren's life. His demeanor and comportment changed around the office. It was as if he had lost his best friend sometimes. She wanted to step right in and fill that void, but Darren always shut the door on her. Invitations to dinner and neck massages in the office to help alleviate his stress were offered daily by Abigail, but Darren stood his ground and denied her services and invitations. He wanted to keep their relationship professional.

Tina had it coming, though. She was talking about how she felt like she had been neglecting Darren's needs during her brother's tumultuous moments, to her girlfriend on the phone, and how she needed to bring the excitement back into their relationship. She only fell short of saying she hadn't been a good wife. Her conscience was eating at her. Darren was eavesdropping and he wanted to make her feel special. He didn't want her to feel bad because she had to deal with her brother's situation. She didn't necessarily tell her girlfriend the details of what had been going on, but he got the gist of her conversation with her friend, talking about, "You know Darren is my world, and I hope I didn't make him feel neglected while I dealt with my brother's problems. I want to do something special for him to show him that he's my number one. I need to get a little freaky for my man." Her girlfriend was giggling on the other line and told her, "Girl, you know you have a good man in Darren and he appreciates you in more ways than you can imagine. You don't have to worry about him." Tina responded, "I know he appreciates and love me, but I need to make him feel like my husband, and I need to do it with all my heart. I want to make it nice and sweet for him this week." Darren was within earshot of her when she made her statement, but he didn't make his presence known. He had no idea who she was talking to on the phone. He simply smiled to himself and promised he would make her feel very special the next night. Darren already knew his wife loved him dearly. He never questioned her devotion to him. He wanted to help rid her of her guilt, so he decided he would take care of things his way, the following night. It had been a while since Darren brought his creative talents to bedroom, but Tina would find out the next day how creative and exciting her husband could be.

Just when Tina thought she had seen all of Darren's tricks, she came home to find him wearing a policeman's uniform, while waiting for her at the front door with a warrant in his hand that he printed from his computer. "Good evening, ma'am. I'm here to place you under arrest for having a guilty conscience. And because of the nature of your crime, I have been summoned to cuff and blindfold you," Darren told her in his sexiest voice. "But excuse me, officer, what basis do you have for this arrest?" Tina asked as she played along. "Well, according to the complaint on the report, you stated that you wish you could do something nice for your husband, because you have been neglecting him, and that, my dear, is grounds for an arrest. And as a dangerous offender, I have to blindfold you before taking you to the location where you will serve your time," Darren said, while trying to keep a straight face. "Well, I guess you gotta to do what you gotta do, officer. Please be gentle with me," Tina begged. "I need you to extend your arms forward, so I can place these cuffs on you. I'm also going to put the blindfold on you, because you are a security risk." Darren was having fun with the whole situation.

After he cuffed and blindfolded Tina, Darren led her upstairs to the guest room. He didn't want to take her to a usual place, like her bedroom. He wanted to take away her familiarity with the place. Darren proceeded to take off Tina's skirt and ripped her blouse off aggressively. "I'm gonna have to report you to your senior officer, because this blouse is one of my favorites," Tina warned. "Go ahead, file your report, all you're gonna get is more punishment. And I mean a lot of punishment for being a bad girl. I'm sure that blouse is replaceable, but right now, I'm gonna need you to be quiet, Miss, while I get you ready, so you can begin serving your time, right!" Darren told her. Tina had no idea what was going on. Darren spun her around a few times to confuse her a little about the direction they went upstairs in the house. After entering the room and securing the door behind him to make sure the fantasy swing was securely draped over the door, Darren locked it. The fantasy swing had two lower leg straps, so Tina could slide her thighs through the lower loops. The two higher loops gave her the comfort-ability to slide her hands through the loops, while holding on for safety. Since Tina decided not to wear any panties that morning, it made Darren's job a lot easier. Tina had never been on anything like that before, and she wondered what it was. After adjusting the straps to a comfortable height, Darren lifted one of Tina's legs and placed it through the first loop on the swing. He did the same with the other leg. Tina's legs were spread apart like a gymnast, cuffed and blindfolded for the occasion. He handed her the two higher loops so she could hold on for safety with her hands.

Tina anxiously awaited Darren's venom as she hung suspended from the door. "What are you gonna do to me, Officer?" She enquired. "Didn't I ask you to keep your mouth shut? By the time I'm through with you, you're gonna have more charges and more punishment than you can handle," Darren said in a serious tone. Meanwhile, Darren took his hat off and placed it on the guest bed, while taking in the aroma of Tina's hot pink pussy, which was completely exposed, because her legs were spread in a split position. His twelve-inch dick was hard and filled with every ounce of blood his body could produce. Tina could only imagine the sexy view that was before her. Darren took off his shirt, rubbed a strawberry liquid on his chest and moved close enough to Tina so she could slowly run her tongue on his chest. "That was delicious, Mr. Officer. Can I have a little more?" she begged. "Again, Miss, I'm gonna need you to be quiet while I do my job. I really don't want to make your punishment any more severe than it has to be," Darren told her before moving back to stroke his dick, while staring at his wife's naked body and hot pink pussy. Tina looked good and Darren was hungry for her. He took the warm flavored liquid and poured a little bit of it on Tina's clit. The warmth of the liquid filled Tina with anticipation. She was careful not to say anything this time. She wished she could rub a quick nut out, but her hands were cuffed. Darren smiled to himself as Tina tried to maneuver her legs so she could rub her clit with her inner thighs. That Kegel exercise wasn't happening. Tina's pussy was draped with the red liquid, now threatening to hit the carpet on the floor. As the white liquid begin to slowly drip from her pussy, Darren knelt before her and with the quick maneuvering of his tongue, he caught her juices before it hit the floor.

The strawberry flavored liquid tasted good, but it would taste even better with Tina's clit enveloped in it. Admiring time was over; Darren needed to take Tina somewhere she had never been before, sexually. With Tina's legs spread apart, there was no obstruction to

Darren's tongue's short voyage towards her clit. Filled with anticipation, Tina didn't even know when it hit her, Darren started licking her from the top of her clit and down into the depth of her sweet tasting pussy. She wanted to scream, but her commander had warned her to keep quiet. The pleasure of having her husband eat her pussy while being completely bound and submissive to his tongue intensified Tina's curiosity. His tongue felt so good, she couldn't attribute anything but the scenario to the situation. Maybe being suspended in the air caused her pussy and the blood flow to her thighs to be overly sensitive, she thought. It was euphoria at its highest. Tina's body trembled at the flick of Darren's soft tongue over her clit. The excitement from Darren's tongue was intensified by the fact that Tina had no physical control over the situation. As Darren continued to slowly lick from her clit to her anus, Tina's body started to jerk. She knew he was forcing an excruciatingly pleasurable nut out of her. She cocked her head back while she climaxed like she had never done before. Though it was hard for Tina to remain silent, her sulking was enough confirmation for Darren to know he had taken her there.

Darren had just started. After that explosive nut, Tina wondered what was next. Darren moved close enough to her, while leaning his body back far enough, so she couldn't touch him. He took the head of his hardened penis and started rubbing it up and down on Tina's clit. The sensation was almost unbearable because she knew she would come just as fast, again. She started to moan louder with each stroke of his penis against her clit. As her legs shook uncontrollably, Darren teased her more by inserting the head of his penis down to the shaft inside her and then quickly took it out. The large circumference of his mushroom dick always made Tina squirm in pleasure. She started biting her lips, hoping Darren would just stand there and let her have all twelve of his inches at once. He continued to tease her as wetness invaded her pussy. "Fuck that, I'm tired of you teasing me. Will you fuck me already!" she screamed at the top of her lungs. "I told you I'm in control of this, not you. I'm gonna fuck you when I'm ready," Darren told her to raise her angst. He slowly pulled his penis out and inserted his middle finger, as his thumb caressed her clit. The moaning and groaning started again, as Tina grinded over Darren's finger trying to steal a quick nut from his manual stimulation. He could sense she was about to come once more, and slowed down his fingers as she tightened her thighs anticipating a nut just the same.

Darren was done playing games. It was time to punish Tina. He spun her around so she could face the door, while her ass hung suspended in the air in front of him. He spread her ass cheeks as he slowly penetrated her from behind, allowing her to feel every single inch of his dick, until all twelve inches were deep inside her. Tina hopped up and down on his dick, moving her body in all kinds of ways trying to find a comfortable position. While she grinded on him, she felt a sting of fingers across her ass cheeks. It was in accord with the long strokes she was now getting from Darren. "Smack my ass," she begged. "You like that? "He asked as he bent his knees to come up with a longer stroke for her. "Oh yes!" she screamed as the head of his penis made contact with her cervix. "Fuck me hard, baby," she told him as she jumped up and down on his long dick. "Fuck your pussy, baby. It's all yours," she confirmed. "Tell me you love this dick," Darren commanded. "I love this dick! I love this dick! Fuck me, Darren!" His strokes were coming a mile a minute, while he spanked her ass red. Sweat poured down Darren's body as he pummeled Tina from behind. His rock hard dick was digging for gold, as his body started to convulse minutes later. "I'm coming, Tina!" he announced as he hurried his strokes. "Wait, please baby! I wanna come with you," Tina told him. Darren slowed his strokes down and positioned Tina sideways against the door, as he held on to her thigh. "Right there, baby. Right there! Stroke me!" Tina begged. Darren increased the speed of his strokes once more. "You like that?" he asked through clinched teeth as he pounded Tina's pussy with force. "Yes, baby! I'm about to come!" she screamed. Darren held her leg tight as he fucked his nut out of his body in unison with Tina.

The two of them were exhausted. Darren lifted Tina out of the swing and placed her on the bed. He took off her blindfold and handcuffs as the two of them collapsed until the next morning. Tina would never forget that night, because it was a night where she relinquished control to Darren for the first time since they had been together. She definitely enjoyed it and couldn't wait to be controlled again by Darren in the bedroom, soon. "I want you to know that I will always understand that family comes first, and we are family. You don't ever have to worry about me when there's a family crisis to deal with. I love you," Darren said before he fell into a coma.

Chapter 29

Abigail and Tina had become such close friends that she was the first person Tina called in the morning to let her know about Darren's antics in the bedroom the previous night. Darren fucked her so well she needed to tell somebody about it. She trusted Abigail enough as a friend to let out her bedroom secrets to her. Abigail just listened on the phone without saying much. At one point, she pressed the mute button on her phone, so Tina couldn't hear her heavy breathing as she masturbated, while listening to the details that Tina described to her about her husband's performance. Abigail was lying in her bed wearing simply her panties and bra when she first answered the phone. As Tina brought the story to a climactic state, Abigail slowly slid her fingers down her wet panties. Her pussy was a slippery course and she glided her fingers all over her clit as she listened intently to Tina describing Darren's twelve-inch dick penetrating her pussy, while she was tied up in the swing. Abigail's moans and groans were loud, but the mute button shielded her from being exposed. "I can't wait to fuck Darren," she murmured to herself, as Tina talked on. "I only wish you could be there to see for yourself how this man was serving my pussy up," Tina said to Abigail. "Maybe I will get that chance one day, you never know?" Abigail said. Tina was not shy about her sexuality and she might've opened Pandora's Box to Abigail.

Abigail was still working on her nut when she pressed the mute button again, so she could focus. She would say something to Tina every so often to let her know she was still on the line listening, but Tina's story was taking her to a different place. Now with her eyes closed, and her imagination running wild, Abigail positioned Darren in front of her on his desk at work with her legs spread wide open. Each finger she glided inside of her pussy felt like Darren's twelve inches piercing through her wall, as she imagined it. She dug deeper with her fingers and tighten her muscle to feel the stiffness of his imaginary dick. Suddenly, she hit the spot she was reaching for. Abigail started yelling, "Yes! Yes Darren, make me cum!" Her body trembled and her soul was relaxed as she climaxed to the tune of Darren's imaginary voice telling her, "Take it, baby. Take it all. Cum for me, baby."

Tina was long done with her story, and she kept yelling through the phone, "Abigail! Abigail, are you there!" She was in a trance as the river wild came running down her thighs, but she recollected herself, just in time to answer through the receiver, "I think the call almost dropped." It was an acceptable enough of an excuse, so Tina told her she would call her back later. Abigail rolled right over in her bed for a long nap.

Chapter 30

Work just wasn't the same for Abigail that following Monday. She now knew too much about Darren's bedroom skills and it was hard to focus around him. Though she valued her job and friendship with Tina, she considered quitting, making it easier on herself. She could only maintain her friendship with Tina by keeping herself away from Darren, she thought. It was torture to be around a man so kind and so great, but belonged to somebody else. It wasn't fair. There was no other way...unless she came up with a different strategy that could land her the best of both worlds. Abigail needed to come up with a master plan that would land her Darren and still maintain her friendship with Tina. Abigail was also wrestling with her emotions as it related to Darren. She didn't know if she was just infatuated with the idea of fucking him, or if she wanted him for herself. She thought he was a great man, but she wasn't sure if he was a great man for her. Tina heightened the need for her to fulfill a curiosity, because of the stories she kept telling her about her husband. Abigail also realized that there was a possible chance that there was no limit with Tina's sexually. Tina brazenly told her she dated a woman when she was younger, but never considered herself a lesbian. Abigail was also attracted to Tina, but there was never a second thought on pursuing her attraction, at first.

There was no better opportunity for Abigail to pursue her new plans than the time Tina invited her over for an engagement dinner for Will and Cassandra. It was supposed to be a family and close friends gathering, but Tina slipped up and mentioned it to Abigail by accident. She had no choice but to invite her. That night would also mark the shift in Abigail and Tina's friendship. As usual, Abigail used every opportunity to look her best and flaunt her assets, and this night would be no different. The cool autumn temperature offered her the ability to wear something fitted and light enough to highlight her best assets. Abigail looked good in her multi-way, tight-fitting, short gray virgin wool dress that she wore off the shoulder with a sexy pair of stilettos and a silk scarf around her neck to accessorize the dress. Tina took inventory of Abigail's dress when she opened the door to let her inside the house. It was a look of approval that Abigail hadn't seen before. "You look good, chica," Tina said, while hugging Abigail at the front entrance. "You look good, too," Abigail returned the favor and smacked Tina on the butt as she turned to walk back towards the dining room, where the rest of the party attendees were waiting. Tina was strutting her stuff like she was flirting with Abigail.

The situation could've been awkward for Abigail if she and Will had clicked when Tina and Darren attempted to hook them up, but everything was cool because Will's fiancée was gorgeous and looked good in every way. He had his eyes focused on her. If anything, Abigail looked so good, Darren found it hard to keep his eyes off her. It wasn't the type of dress that Abigail could wear in the office. Her curves were very well accentuated and her makeup was flawless. Abigail was a head-turner that evening. Even Tina found herself locking lustful eyes with

Abigail, most of the night. Tina tried her best to replicate what her mother did when she had the dinner party for Will after he was exonerated from his charges, but she came up a little short. Still, her efforts were appreciated. She was nowhere near as good a cook as her mother was. The sweet potato pie was bought from the supermarket and she relied on a few frozen pre-cooked items to pull off her dinner. Nonetheless, everyone showed their appreciation through compliments, and the food actually came out great. Tina was still learning her way around the kitchen and she received encouragement from her husband every time she tried. The celebration went accordingly and everyone was having a good time.

After dinner, Abigail offered to help Tina wash the dishes and tidy up the kitchen. Tina was more than happy to have a companion in the kitchen with her. Her parents were a little tired as they had a long drive back to their home in Long Island, so they left early. A few other guests made their way out the door after congratulatory hugs to Will and his new bride-to-be. Some people brought gifts and the couple happily opened the gifts and thanked everyone for their generosity. Ray Ray soon left because he had an early meeting the next day. It was odd that Tina didn't even try to hook up Abigail with her cousin Ray Ray. He was single and so was she. Since he didn't ask any questions about her, she didn't bring it up. But she caught him watching her with lustful eyes a few times.

The room was almost cleared when Tina decided to walk away to the kitchen to clean up. Cassandra also offered to help her, but Tina quickly shut her down. "This is your night. You stay here with Will and Darren and enjoy yourself. Don't worry about me. Besides, Abigail is plenty of help. Just relax and have a good time. Darren, Will and Cassandra remained in the family room watching some documentary on the Civil Rights Movement on PBS. The three of them were discussing and expressing their feelings about the mistreatment of black folks in the '50's and '60's. It was an engaging conversation. Meanwhile, Tina and Abigail were in the kitchen keeping busy. Every once in while, Tina would go to the family room to check on everybody.

By the end of the night, something about Abigail and Tina's relationship had completely changed. There was a look of guilt on Tina's face, but she tried her best to hide it from her husband and the other two guests. Abigail left before Will and Cassandra. Tina walked her to her car after she said goodbye to the other people in the house. Soon after, Will and Cassandra also left to go back to his parents' house in Long island. Tina and Darren were beat and it was time to call it a night.

Chapter 31

That night, Tina went to bed with naughty thoughts on her mind. It was midway through the night when Tina stuck her ass up in the air, while her face was buried in the pillow and her hands gripping the sheet. Her pussy was being licked from behind and she didn't want it to stop, in her wet dream. "Lick my pussy, baby," she cooed as the snake tongue was buried deep inside her pussy cavities. Light smacks across her ass only increased her need to climax, but the oral voyage had just begun. "Oh my God, you eat my pussy so well, baby," she cried out. The soothing hands caressing her back and palming her ass, only added to Tina's pleasure. "Stick your tongue deep inside my pussy," she begged. Tina's eyes were shut tight as she dreamed about Abigail eating her pussy like no one had done before, but Darren, lying next to her, thought Tina's wet dream was all about him. Tina's moans awoke him from his sleep. Whatever she was dreaming about, he was willing to make it a reality. When she nudged him with her elbow in the middle of the night with her finger buried in her pussy screaming, "Eat my pussy, baby," Darren had no choice but to wake up and obey Tina's orders. He turned and shook his head while looking at his wife playing with her pussy in her sleep. Tina was on her back for a long while as Darren ate her pussy in her sleep. Her dripping hot pussy drove him wild. He stuck his tongue in and out it until she rolled to her knees to stick her ass up with her cheeks spread so he could eat her from behind.

All the while, Tina's wet dream had nothing at all to do with her husband. Her fantasy about making out with the beautiful Abigail transformed into a dream. "Kiss me with those soft lips," she begged. She ran her fingers through Abigail's hair and started sucking on her breasts. Abigail's breasts were nice, firm and round. Tina took them in her mouth one at a time. The way she gently caressed his breasts almost sent Darren into a confused state. She had never been that gentle with him in the past. Maybe she was a lot gentler in her dreams, he thought. To Tina, it was Abigail who stood before her and she treated her as gentle as a woman could. Darren continued to pierce Tina's pussy with his tongue, as she grinded all over his face. She was now on her back with her legs up in the air talking about, "Take my pussy, baby." Darren smiled because even in her sleep Tina was a freak. He stuck a couple of fingers in her pussy as she grinded hard on him. It was time for Darren to bring it home with Tina's favorite tool, his dick. He scooped down between her legs and slowly penetrated her. His slow grinds got her pussy dripping wet. In her dreams, Tina thought Abigail's fingers inside her pussy were the sweetest thing. She continued to grind on Darren's dick, all the while positioning herself to cum. He helped by remaining still as she searched for the best position to cum. "Here it is, baby!" she announced while cumming. Tina was shocked to find Darren's dick inside of her when she opened her eyes from her wet dream. She came all over his dick. She wondered if she had given away her secret, but Darren was just happy that she allowed him to bust a nut of his own. After an exhausting session, the two of them fell asleep again in each other's arms.

Tina had thought her days of being with a woman was behind her, until that fateful night when Abigail was in the kitchen helping her with the dishes after dinner. While Darren, Cassandra and Will were in the family room watching television, Abigail and Tina took the opportunity to get to know each other a little better. Tina's fears of Darren possibly sleeping with Abigail was erased when Abigail planted a kiss on the lips of a very flirtatious Tina in the kitchen. It was reminiscent of the days when she dated Tracey. For some reason her body yearned for Abigail's touch and Abigail read her body language just right. She planted little kisses up and down Tina's neck, while keeping an eye out for any possible onlookers from the family room. They were like two pubescent teens sneaking around and displaying devious behavior right under their parents' eyes.

The more they fooled around, the bolder Abigail became. Tina found herself leaning against the kitchen cabinet with her legs spread and Abigail's finger invading her pussy while she kissed her. The sound of the loud television was enough to drown out her moans and groans. The fact that Darren, Will and Cassandra were so caught up and angry about the footage of dogs biting black citizens and by firefighters water hosing marchers, gave Tina and Abigail the opportunity to fool around freely with each other. Abigail's supple lips took Tina to another place that night. She was no doubt in love with her husband, but Tina wanted to be touched and satisfied in a different way. Abigail left her with a drenched pussy that night and Tina wondered how much better could it possibly get? She couldn't wait to find out. After all, cheating on her husband with a woman was forgivable, she thought.

Chapter 32

Tina's conscience was eating away at her. She had hoped she didn't say anything to implicate herself in an awkward situation that she would have to explain to her husband. Not long ago, Darren had a wet dream of his own about Abigail, only to wake up with Tina finishing off his dream for him, but he didn't make that connection to Tina's dream. As far as he was concerned, his wife only dreamed about him. It was that confidence that led to Tina and Abigail's sexual relationship right under Darren's eyes. Abigail and Tina were acting a little suspicious around Darren, but he didn't know why. Abigail was no longer flirting with him in the office. She tried as much as she could to keep her distance from him. Now, Tina avoided bringing up Abigail's name as much as possible in conversations. Though Darren didn't make note of it, their behavior was a little peculiar. Still, he didn't make the connection.

Abigail was now dominating the thoughts and dreams of Tina and Darren daily. What were they going to do about it? It was Monday morning and Darren was headed to a seminar for tax preparers where he was encouraged to bring his own presentation to share with the group. Because there was going to be so many people there, they asked everyone to record their presentation beforehand, so they could show it to the audience on a projector. Darren had done his over the weekend, but left the tape in the camera that was sitting on the shelf in the guest room closet. He went to retrieve the tape before leaving the house, but while his hand reached up to grab the camera, his cell phone rang. It was Abigail calling to find out if he was coming in for the day and what time, because he had told her about the seminar the week before. Though Darren's hand was already placed on the camera and accidentally turned it on, by the end of the conversation, he had completely forgotten to take it with him. The distraction on the phone caused him to forget the camera. He hurriedly left the house because he was running late. He grabbed his briefcase, a bagel in one hand and a small file folder in the other hand. He realized he left his presentation behind when he arrived at the conference.

As an accountant, Darren was quite meticulous. He always backed up everything he did, either through email or a flash drive. Luckily he forwarded the presentation to his email to view it before presenting at the seminar. Though he wanted to make some edits to his presentation, which is why he had put the memory card back in the camera, he had to forgo those edits because the raw footage was all that he had. It was no sweat; he was able to download his presentation into a back-up flash drive that he carried in his briefcase at all times. Darren's presentation on maximizing clients' portfolio was a hit at the seminar, which consisted mostly of white CPA's (Certified Public Accountants) and MBA's (Masters in Business Administration). He received a standing ovation and answered questions during a Q&A session. Everyone was impressed. Darren also learned a few things from his colleagues at that seminar that would help enhance his business that now grew to a full fledge financial services firm, which included investments, life insurance as well as tax preparation. Darren also acquired his 7 series license and a brokerage license, which certified him as a broker of stocks, bonds and other products and complete financial services.

It was a long day and an expensive seminar, but it was all worth it. Darren called his office around noon to tell Abigail that he wasn't returning to the office. He told her he might be at the seminar until the late hours of the evening, possibly around nine o'clock that night. The seminar was scheduled to end at nine o'clock that evening, but Darren had planned to stay until three o'clock for a few sessions he thought were important to his business. However, when he got there, he realized there were more sessions he needed to attend. He stuck around until seven o'clock that evening to attend a seminar on real-estate investment trusts (REITS). It was something that Darren was hoping to bring to his firm and make it available to his clients. The rest of the seminar sessions were subjects that Darren had already mastered.

Chapter 33

When Tina called the office to tell Abigail about her dream, the thought of inviting her over to her house never crossed her mind. Abigail picked up the phone right away when it rang. She noticed Darren's home number on the caller ID. She thought he had made it back home early and was calling to let her know, but it was Tina on the phone. "How are you?" Tina asked when Abigail picked up the phone. Now her voice was filled with excitement when she heard Tina's voice. "I'm doing much better now," she said. She wanted to see Tina again, and Tina secretly had a crush on her too. "I know my husband is attending a conference today, so why don't you close the office a little early and come by for a couple of hours?" Tina suggested. Some things didn't need to be repeated, and in this case, Tina didn't have to ask twice. Abigail jumped at the opportunity to see Tina again. It was around three thirty in the afternoon when she decided to close the office and forwarded all calls to her cell phone. She drove straight to Tina's house, filled with excitement, without knowing what to expect. The only thing she knew was that she and Tina were going to be alone, and last time they were together, things got heated between them in the kitchen.

Tina didn't anticipate Abigail's tongue to move so sensually between her inner thighs, before she attacked her labia and clit, making her nice and wet. Abigail continued sucking and licking her clit to increase her stimulation and the possibility of a quick ejaculating orgasm out of Tina.

She then stuck her index finger inside Tina's pussy as her tongue explored her pussy lips and clit. As Abigail stuck her newly manicured fingers in her mouth before inserting them back in Tina's pussy for stimulation, Tina was lost in her beauty and the lust in her eyes was apparent. "Lick my pussy," she screamed to the point where she was almost about to cum, but she regained control of herself and continued to enjoy the glistening wet effect that Abigail had sprung on her pussy. Tina was hot and ready to go.

Abigail continued to slide her index and middle fingers in and out of Tina's pussy firmly and slowly, touching her wall with the tip of her fingers. She applied just enough pressure to get Tina to shout, "Oh shit! You're gonna make me cum." Tina's pussy was drenched and her muscles loosened as Abigail licked every nook and cranny her tongue could find around Tina's crotch area. Tina was just about ready to have a mind-blowing orgasm when Abigail pulled back to keep her from cumming too quickly. Abigail wanted to make sure that Tina came in the most unique way, not the way Darren made her cum the other night that she kept bragging about. She maneuvered her fingers around inside Tina's pussy, touching every erogenous area she could find, until she hit her G-Spot. Towards the entrance of Tina's pussy, she went back and forth with her fingers as she searched for Tina's inner wall where a rougher patch of skin lay. Tina started grinding on her fingers as Abigail held her hand steady, because she knew she had accomplished her mission to find Tina's G-Spot. "Oh my God!" Tina screamed as her pussy gave in to the pleasure of Abigail's fingers. "I'm cumming! Yes, I'm cumming!" she yelled, boosting Abigail's ego. Satisfied, she knew exactly how to please Tina. There was no turning back now. She wanted this experience to have some type of permanency and not just a once in a lifetime moment.

Making Tina feel good was one thing, but Abigail wanted to see her squirm. After taking a short break from their last session, Abigail was about to hit Tina with all her tricks. Now that she had found Tina's G-Spot, she knew exactly where to go to elevate Tina's breathing within minutes. Tina's pussy was still wet and Abigail needed no lubrication to slide her fingers back inside Tina's pussy to create a rhythm that started a moaning session that Abigail was silently chuckling at. Tina was the kind of freak that Abigail had been searching for, but she wasn't an available woman. Still, Abigail never gave up hope. A freak like Tina needed someone that can make her cum at will, she thought. Abigail mounted Tina and started riding her like she was riding a dick. The friction of clit rubbing against clit surprisingly forced a quick orgasm out Tina. The look on Tina's face said it all. Abigail also experienced an orgasm of her own. Tina couldn't believe she was being turned out by her husband's shy assistant. Tina had never squirted before, but all that was about to change. Abigail buried her tongue between Tina's legs, and she used techniques that Tina had never been subjected to before, to make her cum. As Abigail's fingers smoothly rubbed Tina's G-spot to a nice rhythm, her tongue was wreaking havoc to her clit. Tina couldn't believe it. Cumming had never felt so good to her. She grabbed the pillow, Abigail's hair and anything else for comfort as Abigail ate her pussy and finger-fucked her until she felt she needed to pee, but she was wrong. The clear liquid exiting Tina's pussy, while Abigail licked her clit and finger fucked her, was nothing but an earth-shattering and mind-blowing orgasm that forced her to squirt. Tina had no idea there were so many ways to cum. She just had to be with the right partner. Tina almost passed out after cumming so intensely, but she knew she couldn't risk getting caught in the guestroom in bed with Abigail by her husband. The two of them got up and took a shower together before she sent Abigail on her way.

Chapter 34

Darren couldn't believe his eyes. He had to shake himself out of the trance that he thought he was in. There was no possible way that his wife was sexing his assistant. They were good friends and that was all, he wanted to believe. But the tape didn't lie. Every single action was captured on the camera that Darren accidentally left on record that morning before he left the house. In a haste to make it to his seminar on time, Darren accidentally pressed the record button on his video camera. He left it behind on the shelf, and accidentally positioned it to record every single move made by Abigail and Tina on the bed in the guestroom. Tina had no idea her tryst with Abigail in the guestroom was caught on camera. Out of respect for their bedroom and the sanctity of marriage, Tina thought the guestroom would be the perfect place to have her sexual tryst with Abigail. It all started downstairs on the couch where Abigail picked up where she left off in the kitchen the night of the dinner for Will's engagement. Her soft lips and sensual kisses drove Tina crazy. She wanted to move to a more comfortable setting. The queen size bed in the guestroom gave them plenty of space to roll around, but little did she know, everything was being captured on the camera.

It wasn't until they moved to the bathroom, away from the guest room, that their actions were off camera. Darren shook his head and couldn't believe that his assistant and his wife were fooling around behind his back. Though he was angry, he now had reasons to validate sleeping with Abigail, something he tried to avoid since she started working for him. However, things would take a different direction in the office. Tina was about to be exposed to a different shade of Darren, since she had exposed a new shade of her own. Tina had crossed the line and broken her marriage vow. Darren could've acted hastily and confronted Tina with the tape, but he was in love with his wife and he didn't want to divorce her. He found the tape rather sexy, but he now he had a weapon in his arsenal to use against Tina, should she get out of line. Video proof of cheating was a dream comes true for any spouse in a relationship, and Darren planned to use it accordingly, if he had to.

Darren went to work that morning and acted as normal as he possibly could with Abigail, as he also did the same at home with Tina. Neither of them came clean. He wondered how long they both could keep the truth from him. He didn't press either of them. However, he also received a phone call that morning from his attorney about the discrimination case that he had filed against the white building owner who had refused to rent to him, and it was the best news he had received in a long time. His attorney informed him that the landlord decided to settle out of court with him for almost a quarter of a million dollars. Darren had filed a multi-million dollar lawsuit against the landlord when he learned that the man had been practicing racial discrimination across the state. His lawyer found out the building owner also owned commercial properties all across New York State and he was worth millions of dollars. Darren and his lawyers decided it was time to put a stop to his discriminatory practices. Darren was jumping for joy when his lawyer informed him that other victims came forward and the landlord stood to lose everything he owned if he didn't settle the case, which had now become a class-action lawsuit that involved many different minority victims. Darren was jumping around in a celebratory mood, Abigail asked him, "What are you so happy about?" with a smile on her face. He inadvertently kissed her on the lips and unanticipated the kiss becoming more passionate as he held on to her lips longer. She kissed him right back. As a matter of fact, when he tried to pull away from her, she held on to his lips with her lips and continued to softly suck on them. This was the moment Abigail had been waiting for.

      Without thinking, Darren cleared his desk and sat Abigail on the edge of it. Their lips never disconnected. Abigail rushed to get his tie off as she kissed him. She wanted to run her hands across his bare chest. After taking off his tie, she knew exactly where it was headed. It was too late to stop. He helped her get his shirt off. Though Darren had not been to the gym in a while, the push-ups he did at his house helped him keep his beautiful physique. Abigail was delighted at his biceps after she took off his shirt. The only pieces of clothing left to take off were his undershirt, underwear and pants. By now, Abigail's blouse was fully unbuttoned and her perky breasts were just waiting to be sucked by Darren. Her dark berry-looking nipples looked delightful. She continued to pull off pieces of his clothing one by one. She started to fan herself at his exposed chest. No words were exchanged between the two of them, as they pursued lust in its most silently awkward way. Everything they wanted to say to each other was spoken through their eyes and their physical action.

Abigail had been waiting for this day and Darren wished it hadn't come to this, but now, he was able to do what he was doing without feeling much guilt. It was his own way of paying his wife back, but still, Abigail was in the middle of it all. What was going to happen after this? Would they be able to maintain a professional relationship? Would this go on forever? These were some of the questions that Darren and Abigail never stopped to think about. The only thing in their minds at the time was the collision of his dick inside her pussy. The connection of flesh was all that mattered, even for a passionate moment where regrets could come at a later time. Abigail and Darren were willing to be selfish, in order to satisfy their lustful curiosities.

She ran her fingers up and down his six-pack abs and up to his pecks, where she placed her soft tongue and suckled on his nipples. The forbidden passion never felt so good, as new pussy has always been the Achilles' heel for most men, or something like kryptonite to Superman. Darren was neither super nor was he acting like a real man at the time, as he stared into the beautiful eyes of Abigail, while she attempted to take him to a place he had been imagining in his head for the last few months. Her beautiful chocolate face made it even harder for him to grow a conscience. He couldn't ask her to stop. She was breathtaking that morning when she walked into the office wearing a black miniskirt, unusual four-inch heels, a fitted white shirt and her hair down. Darren noticed every single curve on her body that morning. He had never paid so much close attention to her before. Perhaps his action was precipitated by the action of his wife on that tape. Darren's eyes were lustful and Abigail took notice. Though she had hoped he would act on his lust, she never though he would be ballsy enough to pursue her. As a boss, Darren never even took the time to think about the door he was leaving wide open for a possible lawsuit for sexual harassment by his assistant. His dick was doing all the thinking and that was all that mattered at the time.

No longer concerned with Tina's feelings, Darren planned on putting it down hard on Abigail. Her welcoming body and eyes were begging for Darren's voracious actions. It was a moment so awkward, only body language was deemed appropriate for communication. What would they say to each other? What were they even thinking besides lust? They were both guilty, but Abigail even more so, because she had fucked Darren's wife. Was Abigail a younger version of Tina? Perhaps! Those consequences and comparisons didn't matter. Darren reached to softly caress Abigail's breasts with his hands. They were firm, like his wife's. Her protruded nipples were hard. He took them in his mouth one at a time, sucking on them gently. His sensitive touch transformed her pussy to the equivalent of Niagara Falls, in terms of the flow of her juices. His every touch excited every part of her body, including her mind. The man she had come to know in the past couple of years or so was everything she had imagined. His subtle and sweet touches drove her wild. His soft kiss was the aphrodisiac that drove her sexual yearning. "Fuck me. Fuck me hard!" she wanted to say, but her silence was golden. He could read her body language, understood and knew her needs and wants at the time. He wanted to fuck her, not just to fulfill his own fantasy, but to make sure his actions will be worth the possible punishment that lay ahead.

Abigail was obviously a gym rat, because her abs were just as tight as Darren's. He ran his tongue down her washboard leisurely. Her head was cocked back, hands gripped the front edge of the desk tightly, while she enjoyed the feel of his soft tongue against her body. He slowly slid her thong underwear down her smooth shaven legs. He pushed her body back towards the middle of the desk with her legs spread wide open. Her pussy lips had a purplish hue, but deep inside, he could see pinkness, and it was nicely manicured. She had a little landing strip right above her clit. Perfect, he thought before bending down to bury his face between her legs. "Mmmmh," he mumbled for the first time. He was either taking a long whiff of her sweet smelling pussy or the anticipation of his tongue buried deep inside her pussy, forced the words out of his mouth. Either way, Abigail soon felt her clit vibrating softly as Darren slowly erected it with his tongue. Her moans and groans exuded from her body without any self-control. Darren was as good as Tina told her, she thought. Her purplish-pink pussy looked appetizing as he entombed his tongue deep inside her. Her nectar was as sweet as water to a thirsty man. He went in and out with his tongue as her legs shook around neck. Abigail was reaching the point of no return and Darren felt it coming. He reached up to massage her breast with one hand, while one of his fingers from his other hand lay on her clit in a circular motion. His tongue never wavered and Abigail couldn't help it. "I'm cumming!" she screamed as she held on tight to the desk. Her body jerked back and forth, and she continued to shake until it was too sensitive for Darren to keep his finger on her clit anymore. Mission accomplished. Abigail came.

Darren still had a chance to be off the hook, if he had just walked away. He could've acted like President Clinton and make the claim to his wife that he did not have sex with his assistant. Oral sex is not considered sex to most men. The first lady seemed to have accepted that excuse from the President, so why not him? he thought. However, there remained a problem with his hard dick looking for a hole to regurgitate the white, thick semen that was screaming to come out of his body. Darren had already gone too far, there was no turning back. Besides, Abigail hungered for that twelve-inch dick. That's all she had been dreaming about since Tina mentioned it to her. She wanted it and she wanted it in her mouth, her pussy and wherever else he wanted to put it. Still wearing his pants, the imprint of Darren's big dick was mouth-watering to Abigail. She stopped salivating long enough to reach for it. Finally, she had the golden dick in her hand. What was the first thing she was gonna do with it? She pulled it out of his pants and thought, 'that's a beautiful dick.' The vein-filled, chocolate, thick dick belonged in her mouth. "Fuck Tina!" she said to herself in her moment of selfishness. The friendship couldn't have meant that much to her anyway, otherwise she wouldn't be holding Tina's husband dick in her hands. Tina had it coming for letting her eat her pussy and fucked the hell out of her the way she did, she wanted to force herself to believe.

This was Abigail's time. No one was going to stop her shining. She needed that moment with Darren, even if it meant the friendship with Tina would be over. This was the first time that Abigail had laid eyes on a dick that looked so delicious to her. Twelve inches of pleasure was a lot. Darren stood back and watched Abigail's smiling face as she stroked his dick back and forth with her hand. She licked her lips a few times before jumping off the desk to switch places with him. Still, no words were exchanged. Their body language was enough for them to comprehend each other's next move. Darren's underwear and pants were down to his knees as his feet dangled off the desk. His dick stood right up, almost near his chest, nice thick, long and appetizing to Abigail. She coyly pulled his underwear and pants past his ankles, while pulling off his moccasin shoes. Darren was now sitting butt naked on his desk and Abigail stood before him in all her nakedness staring at him with hungry eyes.

Abigail felt like she needed to do some warm-ups to loosen up her jaws before wrapping her tongue around Darren's big dick. "Tina was not bragging," she said to herself at the site of Darren's dick. Wow, she thought. "How do I suck thee? Let me count the ways," she said in her head. Abigail moved in and grabbed a good four inches of Darren's hard dick in her hand. "Mmmm......nice," she finally said. Darren sat on the desk with his eyes closed anticipating the warmth of Abigail's mouth wrapped around his dick. But Abigail wanted to admire his dick for a little while longer. She kept stroking it back and forth and planted kisses all over it. Darren never once stopped to think about the difference between Abigail's warm mouth and his wife's. Was her mouth that much better? Was Abigail going to blow his dick out of this world? Did she have some dick-sucking skills he hadn't seen before? It was all in his mind, but it didn't matter. Abigail finally took the huge dick in her mouth slowly and allowed her tongue to climb up and down the full length of his dick, like a stripper on a pole. She took forever to get from the base of his dick to the top with her tongue. She ran her tongue slowly over every popping vein on his erected dick, and when she got to the shaft, she circled her tongue around it before filling her mouth with the head. A nice delicious dick was all Abigail ever wanted to taste from Darren.

As Abigail applied suction to the head of Darren's dick, he reached for the back of her head. The feeling was heavenly. He wanted to fuck her mouth. He humped her mouth a few times, while holding back to keep from cumming too soon. He wanted to enjoy every minute of her efforts. As far as he was concerned, he was already at the point of no return and there was no reason not to enjoy it. Abigail had skills. She cocked her head to the side and worked her tongue until he relinquished his strength, control and power. He was like putty in her hand as his semen spilled out of his dick uncontrollably. She downed every drop of it. Darren sat there shaking a few times with his eyes closed. By the time he opened his eyes, Abigail was standing butt naked in front of him in her heels with a condom in her hand. Normally, a recovery period would be necessary, but the sexy goddess standing before him regenerated blood from all over his body back down to his dick. Abigail was a safe bet. She knew one day she would land her man, so she carried a pack of condoms with her, just in case.

Darren and Abigail were so caught up in the moment, they had completely forgotten about the unlocked front door to the office. They were both too concerned with their sexual wants to think about the fact that someone may walk in on them. The safety behind the closed door to Darren's office was enough. However, Tina decided to show up unexpectedly at the office to take her husband to lunch that day. She had just put the car in park and was checking her lipstick on the rearview mirror to make sure she looked good enough for her husband. It had been a while since Tina and Darren ate lunch together. She was hoping for a pleasantly surprised look on his face. As Tina gathered herself in the car, Abigail was just bending over on the desk in front of Darren, waiting to be penetrated from behind. The extra large Magnum condom was rolled all the way to the base of Darren's dick and Abigail braced herself for the piercing of his dick into her tight pussy. He parted her purplish pussy lips with his fingers to gain access to her canal. He slowly pushed himself in and the warmth of her wet pussy enveloped his dick. It felt like heaven, but hell was sitting in front of his office in her car, waiting to bust in on them.

Darren's sweet strokes kept Abigail's moan down to a low sexy tone. She was fueling him. His hands rested on her tiny waist, and her thighs just provoked his desire to fuck her well. Darren was finally in the pussy. Meanwhile, Tina was just reaching across to the seat to grab her purse, so she could get out of her car to go surprise her husband. However, her phone rang. At first, she didn't want to pick it up, but it was her dad calling from the office. "Hi dad, I'm at lunch," she said right away when she picked up the phone. "I know, honey, but I need you to run to this jobsite for me, because one of my contractors had an emergency and the AC unit is on its way to be delivered. You know if we leave it outside someone's going to steal it. I can't afford to let a $4,000.00 unit go to waste. Please hurry. The guy should be there in fifteen minutes," her father said. Tina had never disappointed her dad and she wasn't about to start. Her status as daddy's little girl was going to remain intact. Daddy saved the day for Darren, when Tina decided to save the day for daddy. Tina started her car right up and backed out of the parking lot to go meet with the people delivering the air conditioning unit, without even letting Darren know she was just in front of his door.

Everything happens for a reason and Darren had plenty of reasons to want to tear up Abigail's pussy. First of all, she was fine beyond belief, and second of all, Tina crossed that line behind his back. It was a form of payback, as far as he was concerned. Darren was ten inch deep inside Abigail's overly drenched pussy. The silence was gone. Abigail was now lying on her back on Darren's desk. Her moans and groans got louder and her ass was moving like a top on the desk, trying to scoop as much dick as possible. Finally, Darren went all the way in, with his balls barely hanging out above her asshole. The friction of his dick flapping back and forth could be heard by anybody within earshot. Darren was banging the hell out of Abigail. "Fuck me, baby!" she yelled like she was familiar with him. Her begging was reminiscent of Tina's, but that was as far as the similarities went. This was new pussy to Darren. He brought Abigail's legs straight up against his chest, so she could feel all twelve of his inches deep down in her crevice. "You're gonna make me cum," she told him. "Cum for me, baby," he told her. Darren stroked her a few more times before his own nut emerged, but Abigail had already experienced rhapsody from his thrusts.

Afterwards, the two of them got dressed and returned to their work. They barely said anything to each other during the rest of the day. They both had a happy look on their faces, but Darren almost had a heart attack when Tina called him to tell him she was in front of his office about a half hour earlier. He wondered whether she had heard the commotion between him and Abigail, but she made no mention of it. However, the guilt was killing him!

Chapter 35

A few weeks had gone by since the tryst between Abigail and Darren took place. That moment of passion brought to the surface feelings that Abigail didn't know existed for Darren. She also felt the same way about Tina. Abigail had tried all her life to pick a team, a side or sexual orientation, but she struggled with it. Deep down, she knew she was bisexual and there was nothing that she could do about it. Though Abigail never wanted the stigma of homosexuality to be attached to her as a person, society in general always assumes same-sex couples are homosexual. In high school, Abigail tried to suppress her feelings for women, but it was a fight she could not win. She was also attracted to some of the handsome guys at her school, especially the athletic types. There was no problem when it came to her attraction to the men, because it was acceptable to be heterosexual. She didn't even have to hide that fact from her parents. Bringing a boy home to meet her parents was as normal as normal could be. Abigail, however, was also bringing home her "girlfriend." Her parents had no idea Abigail had a thing for women. There was no supervision when she was in her bedroom with her girlfriend. Her parents trusted that they were doing girly things. It was her parents' trust that afforded Abigail the opportunity to get sexual with a woman when she was only fifteen years old.

Abigail's friend was a year older with a lot more experience. She was also a lesbian. There was no questioning her sexuality. She liked women, but Abigail's parents thought she was going through a Tomboyish faze when Abigail brought her home. As the friendship between the two girls accelerated, Abigail's friend, Trisha, started coming around more and more. She wore baggy clothes, sneakers and carried herself like boy, but she was the prettiest girlfriend Abigail had ever introduced to her parents. Her younger brother had a huge crush on Trisha, but Trisha had her eyes on Abigail. The slim, light skinned girl, with long curly, beautiful smile and a flat chest was lovable to everybody. Trisha knew exactly what she wanted from Abigail when she first met her. Abigail thought Trisha was so pretty the first day they met in school. They instantly became friends. Abigail was going through the teenage phase when she could not stand boys. She took that opportunity to bond with Trisha. Their friendship blossomed. The first time Trisha stole a kiss from Abigail, it was a shocking moment for both of them. Though Trisha seemed like she regretted making the move on her friend, she was always curious about Abigail. They took baby steps before deciding to finally go all the way one day. After that, Trisha and Abigail were fooling around every day in Abigail's room. The loud music always drowned out any suspicious sound that was coming from the room, and Abigail always locked her door, under the false pretense that she needed peace to do her homework.

Alfred Kinsey's research on human sexuality also brought about his famous Alfred Kinsey's Scale, which suggested that people fall between 0 (totally heterosexual) and 6 (totally homosexual) on a sexual "preference" continuum, meaning homosexuality and heterosexuality are not opposites. Many researchers have found that many people have transitional phases as it relates to their coming out process as bisexual, whether straight or gay. Bisexuals are no different than bi-racial children when it comes to society's perception of them. They're not accepted by straight or gay people. While most people believe the perpetuated myth that bisexuality is a phase in a person's life, Abigail knew since high school she was bisexual, and also knew it would be her lifetime sexual orientation. Abigail became a student of Alfred Kinsey's work when she discovered her bisexuality. She almost attended Indiana University because The Kinsey Institute for Research in Sex, Gender and Reproduction was founded there by Alfred Kinsey, while he was a professor teaching entomology and zoology. Abigail became fascinated with the whole idea of wanting to be with both, a man and a woman. In the depth of her heart, at times, she wished it was just a phase that she was going through, but her capacity for physical, emotional and romantic attraction to both genders couldn't be tamed. So, she had to accept who she is as a person.

Never before had Abigail been attracted to a married couple. In fact, she never intended to take this poly-amorous ride she was taking. She was monogamous all of her life. She either dated a man or a woman, but never both at the same time. Abigail went to bed at night thinking about Darren and Tina. In a perfect world, she would be with both of them, indefinitely. But Abigail knew it was just a fantasy not meant to become a reality. Her love for both of them was equal. No one tipped the love scale more in either direction. She had no idea how this was going to play out.

However, she thought she was the only one who knew that she had been with both of them.

Chapter 36

Darren and Tina acted strange around each other for a while. They were both trying to overcompensate for their guilt of cheating. Darren catered to Tina's every need and Tina did the same for him. Neither of them understood the over-abundance of love and kindness that came from them both. Hot sex was always on the platter. Darren was never too tired to have sex with Tina no matter how late he got home from work. As a matter of fact, he put in extra work to make sure she was satisfied. She reciprocated his every generosity and love. The blowjobs lasted longer and his evening baths became a regular thing. It was just too lovey-dovey in that household. Something had to be done about it. They both ran back into the arms of Abigail. Darren was afraid that he was developing stronger feelings for Abigail. He never questioned his love for Tina, but Abigail brought something different out of him. She soothed his soul in a different way. He continued to have sex with her and even went out on dates with her. He would lie to Tina about conferences and working late at the office, so he could spend time with Abigail. Darren's nose was wide open, but he made it clear to Abigail that he wasn't leaving his wife for her. Darren was also hoping that Abigail would open up to him about the incident that happened between her and Tina, but she never did. She alluded to making a mistake once, but she never delved into the details. He assumed she was talking about the incident with

Tina, but he never pressed for more information than she was willing to offer.

Abigail had developed full-fledged relationships with both Darren and Tina, secretly. She was in love with both of them, because they both treated her well. While Tina may have tried to keep her sexual trysts with Abigail separate from her emotions, she also started to gravitate a little more than she should have and she wondered if it was even possible for her to love two people, Darren and Abigail, at the same time. Darren was wrestling with the same issue. Abigail was no longer just his concubine anymore; he was investing his time in her. He was making long term plans for his company involving her with every detail. Darren and Tina were both now fabricating stories to go spend time with Abigail. Neither of them could complain about the lack of time they were spending with each other, because they were both guilty, but they also knew what was in the dark was eventually going to come to light. It was a matter of time before one of them slipped.

Darren and Tina were both preoccupied with meeting Abigail's need, they never even realized all the effort they were putting into Abigail. As exhausting as cheating was for both of them, they must've both felt Abigail was worth all the trouble.

Chapter 37

Abigail's every need was being met. Tina was the lover that understood and identified with her feminine side. She was also the best friend that Abigail could turn to whenever she needed female perspective or someone to listen to her vent. Abigail became the girlfriend that Tina needed whenever she felt overwhelmed in her marriage. The two of them complemented each other. Now Darren was in the middle. He was the foundation that both women wanted and needed. Darren's attentiveness, caring personality and giving heart was everything the women needed. Both Abigail and Tina wanted and needed him in their lives. Darren also needed them. He had never cheated on his wife before and never thought he ever would, but Darren was at a crossroads where his heart was divided between the two women. There was no scale because Tina was his wife, and he would always choose her over Abigail, but that was not a choice he was willing to make at the time. He wondered how long his relationship with Abigail could go on before he was busted, but Abigail made sure neither of them busted each other. She coordinated all the scheduling of events between them. She didn't want any rift between them. She wanted harmony and peace. Life was wonderful that way. There was no reason to rock the boat or stir the pot. Abigail covered for both of them. They were both cheating on each other because of her. She appreciated their love and the extent they went through to be with her. Abigail only wished their relationship could be out in the open, among all three of them. And she coordinated it exactly that way.

The risk was high, but Abigail had started to grow tired of running behind Darren to see Tina and running behind Tina to see Darren. She wanted to make sure they both knew about the relationship each had with her. She was going to let the chips fall where they may. Though the sexual relationship with Tina and Darren was great for Abigail, she started to yearn for a commitment. It didn't matter if she was with either of them exclusively, but the best scenario was for both of them to agree to be in an open relationship with her. Her decision to bring them together could only have two outcomes: either it would blow up in her face, or she would end up in a relationship that most people only fantasize about, which was to keep the two people she was in love with.

Abigail decided to hold a special dinner for three at her place. She still lived in an apartment in the Jamaica section of Queens, New York. She invited Tina and Darren to her house at seven o'clock and seven thirty respectively, for dinner, but she did not invite them together. She wanted to make sure they didn't run into each other on the way in, so she stressed that they each had to be punctual. Each one received a personal invitation and thought this dinner was going to be an intimate affair for two people, them and Abigail. Both Tina and Darren were excited about their date for later that evening. Each of them was contemplating the best lie to tell each other, so they could get away for the evening. Tina could easily use a visit to go see her mother as an excuse, but she had been using that excuse for a while now. Darren was thinking about using the same lame excuse, but how much time was he really going to spend with his mother? That excuse was wearing thin, for both of them. All day long, Tina and Darren were racking their brains to come up with the best excuse to leave their home that evening. If there was a time Darren needed to have some friends to cover for him; this would be the night. However, Darren had become quite creative since he started seeing Abigail. He decided to tell Tina he was going to check out this new gym he was considering joining. Tina told him she had to meet with a client after hours because the client worked til six o'clock. She needed to go over specifications for a new home her father's company was building for a newlywed couple. It wasn't far-fetched because she had done that in the past. Besides, Darren was looking for his own way out. Who was he to question her commitment for the night?

Since Tina was expected first, at seven o'clock, she was the first to get ready. Her sexy outfit looked a little suspect to be meeting with a client at that time of night, but Darren was looking for his own escape, so he said nothing. He was lying on the couch watching ESPN's Sportcenter, while Tina showered and got dressed upstairs. She threw on an overcoat to shield her sexy dress from Darren. He knew that dress. She had worn it for him in the past. He was so caught up with his own plans he never stopped to think that his wife could possibly be cheating on him with a dude. That was the way his mind was working at the time. He had tunnel vision and his focus was on Abigail for the night. Tina walked by and blew him an air kiss before exiting the house through the kitchen door that led to the garage. She left trails of her sweet smelling perfume throughout the house. Still, Darren hadn't noticed a thing.

Darren ran upstairs the minute Tina's car pulled out of the garage. He had exactly thirty minutes to get ready so he could make it to Abigail's house on time. He was rummaging through his side of the closet to find something fly to wear for Abigail. He settled on a flat-front blue slacks, a fitted sky blue shirt and his favorite brown Crocodile Bit Ferragamo loafers with a brown belt to match. He wore his favorite Panerai, Radiomir mechanical black dial, brown alligator leather watch. He sprayed his favorite Gucci Guilty cologne behind his ears and on his neck. He was ready to serve Abigail on a platter for the night. Darren scrubbed extra hard in the shower that night. He was clean as a whistle, smelled good and looked like a million bucks.

Tina arrived on time as promised. She had to circle the block to find a parking space. She came in smelling as sweet as an imported rose. "You look beautiful as always," Abigail said before moving in for a sweet kiss. Tina kissed her back. She led Tina to the dining room where the table was set for three. "Are we expecting a third person?" Tina asked with curiosity when she noticed the setting of the table. "We are. I have a little surprise for you tonight," Abigail said with a subtle smile. She walked towards the kitchen before Tina could ask her who was coming. "Would you like some wine?" she yelled from the kitchen. "Sure," Tina said back to her. "Red or white wine?" Abigail asked. "What do you have?" Tina asked. "I have a bottle of each in the fridge," she told Tina. "I'll have the red wine. So, when is this friend coming over, and why?" Tina pressed on. "They should be here soon," Abigail revealed. Tina's plan of an intimate night with Abigail wasn't looking so good. She put a lot of effort into her outfit and appearance. She didn't want to share Abigail for the night.

Though the table was set, Abigail hadn't brought the food out yet. She was waiting for Darren to arrive. As always, Darren showed up at exactly seven thirty. He was the most punctual and considerate person she knew, as far as respecting people's time. She went to the door and greeted him with a kiss as well. He handed her a dozen of fresh roses. "These are for you, my dear." Abigail put the roses to her nose and smiled at Darren. He was considerate and consistent, which she liked. "Thank you. You look and smell good," she told him before turning around to head towards the living room where Tina was waiting. The awkward moment was about to be and Abigail could only hope that Tina and Darren acted civil with the whole situation.

Chapter 38

Tina and Darren were shocked to see each other at Abigail's house. "What happened to you meeting a client tonight?" Darren asked with sarcasm in his voice. "I thought you were going to check out a new gym!" Tina yelled out. Abigail could hear the commotion from the kitchen, but she wanted to bring the food out to the table first, before engaging Tina and Darren in a conversation they couldn't have fathomed in their minds. The bickering back and forth between Tina and Darren continued. They were blaming each other for lying. The table was finally set. Abigail encouraged Tina and Darren to get a glass of wine, each. "The reason I invited you both here is because I need to clear the air and I need to let you know how I feel about this situation," Abigail said. Tina and Darren listened intently as she spoke. "I care about both of you. As a matter of fact, I love both of you equally. My dream situation would be to keep both of you in my life, but I already know it's wishful thinking. I even doubt that either of you would be in my life at by end of the night," Abigail said emotionally with a stream of tears running down her face. Darren and Tina both reached over to wipe her tears, Darren on the right and Tina on the left. "This is why I love you both. You guys are thoughtful, sweet, caring, loving and kind-hearted decent people. I have never met anyone like either of you. Maybe that's why you two are married to each other. I never intended to be with both of you, but love can't be controlled. Never in my life have I felt this good. Darren and I fought our attraction for the longest, while working together at the office. I know he respects you as his wife and respects his marriage, but there was a moment of weakness between us and things accelerated to where they are now." Abigail was trying her hardest to make them see her perspective in this three-way relationship.

Abigail then zoomed in on Tina. "From the first time I laid eyes on Tina, I was attracted to her. Though I knew she was married to you, Darren, I couldn't help my attraction to her. As I got to know her, I started developing deeper feelings for her. She's generous, kind, sweet, smart and sexy. She always made me feel special when we went out and she acted like the best friend that I've always wanted. It was me who made the first move on Tina. I took a chance and she was somewhat receptive to it. I couldn't stop thinking about her after that. I had no idea that Tina would even take a second look at a woman, but love has a weird way of manifesting itself. I think all of this happened for a reason. I brought you two here to determine that reason and to see where we're gonna go from this point on." It was a good enough argument and Darren and Tina looked like two confused college applicants waiting to make a decision on which school to attend.

Tina and Darren awkwardly looked at each other. "I would've never had that moment of weakness if I didn't watch Tina and you have sex at my house on my video recorder," Darren spewed out. "Oh, I'm being watched by you now?" Tina asked, trying to flip the script on Darren. "Don't try to turn this thing around on me... and I didn't purposely set up surveillance to catch you. I accidentally pressed the record button on my video camera the morning I was going to my seminar. I was supposed to take the camera with me, but I forgot it. It was when I went back to retrieve the tape that contained my presentation that I noticed Abigail eating the hell outta your pussy and you screaming out the Lord's name!" Darren said heatedly. "So how long have you been keeping this information from me, Darren?" Tina asked like she had any right to be mad with Darren. "It really doesn't matter, Tina. The whole point is that you were seeing Abigail behind my back. I didn't feel any guilt sleeping with her after that, but somewhere along the way, I started to like her more and more and now this. I love you and I think I love Abigail, too. I don't know what the hell to do." Darren shook his head and threw up his hands as he got up to leave. "Darren, sit down! You're not going anywhere until we get this resolved," Abigail said in a commandeering tone. Darren took back his seat.

Tina was feeling ashamed for what she had done. She didn't think Darren knew about her betrayal. She started something that turned into a love triangle. "I'm sorry, Darren. I hadn't thought about being with a woman since Tracey. All I know is that I love you with all my heart and I want to spend the rest of my life with you. My intentions were not to hurt you, but along came Abigail. From the night you brought her over to our house for the hook-up with Will, we had a connection. At the time, I couldn't pinpoint exactly what kind of connection it was, but we eventually explored things and we are where we are now. I have to be honest with you about my feelings for Abigail, because they are strong. I don't want to leave my husband for a woman, but I love Abigail, too. Right now, I think we're all confused about what we should be doing. Maybe we can all sleep on it and figure out a solution in the morning," Tina said. Abigail tried as much as she could to stare deep into the souls of both of them before making her feelings known. "So now, you both get to go home and sort shit out, but I have to be here alone tonight, right? Is that fair to me? My feelings are involved in this too, and I love both of you. I think we should all sleep on this tonight, but we need to do it together in this apartment," she told them in a matter of fact tone. Tina and Darren quickly looked at each other and shook their head in agreement with Abigail. The three of them had dinner and tried to sort out as much of their relationship issues as possible during dinner. By the time Dinner ended, everyone was amicable again.

Chapter 39

Abigail lived in a one bedroom apartment, but she had a standard king size bed, big enough for all three of them to sleep on. Since they didn't bring an overnight bag, Darren and Tina had to sleep in their undergarments. The situation was a little gauche, so Darren volunteered to sleep on the couch in the living room. "If you're sleeping in the living room alone, I could've slept in my bed alone too. I suggested we all stay together tonight, because I want to relish this moment. Just in case it is the last moment of closeness we're ever going to spend with each other, I want it to be memorable. My bed is big enough for all three of us, there's no reason why we shouldn't all be able to sleep on it." Abigail made it clear. She was more assertive than ever.

Tina looked very sexy in her matching black thong underwear and bra. Abigail looked hot in her matching red boy shorts and bra. Darren sported his gray boxer briefs. He lay in the middle of the bed, while Tina was on his right and Abigail on his left. Tina turned to put her head on Darren's chest, as Abigail ran her hands across his stomach. At first, it seemed weird that Darren was lying in the middle of two beautiful women that he cared about, without attempting to do anything to either of them. However, he couldn't fight Mother Nature when Tina became horny. As Abigail ran her hands up and down her husband's body, Tina moved her hands down his crotch to show him that he was still the love of her life. Blood flowed down Darren's dick instantly, as Tina played with his dick. The dim light coming from the street lamp into the room was enough for them to monitor each other's movement. The women needed to make Darren the center of attention. Darren began kissing his wife, as Abigail caressed his back. If there was a heaven, Darren was right in the middle of it, he thought.

Darren felt chills running down his spine as Tina worked her way down from his lips to his stomach. She was delicate. Abigail's hands ran across both of them, soothing them comfortably. "I love you two," she said softly. Abigail wanted to offer Tina and Darren the kind of security needed for them let go their inhibitions. "This love is wonderful and we should explore it to the max," Abigail quipped. Darren turned his head to kiss her. His soft tongue pierced through Abigail's soul. She responded to his kiss passionately. Tina could sense the purity of Abigail's love for Darren. Tina was not going to be neglected, though. Abigail moved down and kissed Tina with the same passion. Now Darren witnessed her true feelings for his wife. Her love for both of them was sealed with a kiss. And they both returned the favor. This wasn't an ordinary threesome where three people were looking to get their freak on; it was love being shared among three people who loved one another. The touching and caressing went on for about ten minutes. Darren tried his best to spread the love equally. Tina did the same. Abigail followed suit.

Darren managed to remove the undergarments for both women. Both women removed his underwear. The vibe between them was great and everyone was comfortable with the situation. All reservation, inhibition and apprehension were laid to rest. Abigail no longer worried about how Tina would react when she demonstrated her love for Darren. She also no longer cared about Darren's reaction when she distributed her love to Tina. Darren and Tina accepted and appreciated all the love that was evoked in the room. Three beautiful naked bodies lay in the bed. And three people with nothing but good loving intentions were breathing each other's air. Tina was the fire-starter to get things started, though. Her tongue found its way to Darren's hardened penis, while Abigail sat on Darren's face, facing the wall. Moans and groans permeated throughout the room. Darren had his tongue in the depth of Abigail's pussy, while Tina had his dick in the depth of her throat. Tina sucked Darren's dick like she had something to prove. She voraciously bobbed her head up and down on his dick, sucking and licking every inch her mouth could muster. She licked his balls, while stroking his dick with her hand, exciting him to the point where he had to control his ejaculation. Darren had just started, and no way was he going to have a false start. He decided to shift his focus on eating Abigail's pussy, making Abigail succumb to his tongue. She held on to the headboard as Darren's tongue found the weakness in her clit. She was winding and grinding fast on his mouth. Unlike Darren, Abigail could enjoy a quick nut and rebound right back. "I'm coming, baby," she blurted out, like she had been there before. Her body shook and Tina watched as her husband made another woman cum in her presence for the first time.

Darren and Tina decided to change positions after Abigail's climactic episode. Tina moved to the center of the bed, on her back, with her legs spread. Darren got between her legs and continued his tongue excursion. At the same time, Abigail started kissing and sucking on Tina's breasts as Darren ate her pussy. Tina ran her fingers through Abigail's hair as the two of them were tightlipped in a passionate kiss that lasted for what seemed forever. Gasps of breaths could be heard in between the kiss. Darren was searching for Tina's spot with his fingers as his tongue manifested itself on her clit. "Eat that pussy, baby," Tina shouted as Abigail found her way to her perky breasts. It was heavenly bliss for Tina. Abigail was yearning to taste her pussy, too. She got on top of Tina with her ass landing on Tina's face and her face on Tina's pussy, in a sixty-nine position. She started licking Tina's clit, as Darren now penetrated Tina. Darren knew the thing Tina loved the most was his big dick. He played with Abigail's hair as he slowly stroked Tina's pussy.

Abigail was working her tongue on Tina's clit, which prompted Tina to smack her ass, while having her own way with Abigail's clit. It was sexual utopia. After every five strokes or so, Darren pulled his dick out of Tina's pussy and stuck it in Abigail's mouth. This went on for a few minutes. Darren could sense that Tina was on the cusp of cumming, when he went deep into her wall, as Abigail played with her clit. He stood his position and allowed Tina to grind her own nut out. "I'm cumming, baby! Oh shit! Keep playing with my clit, Abby. Stand still, Darren. Here it comes!" Tina yelled. Darren and Abigail worked their magic until Tina's body started convulsing. However, they weren't done yet.

Darren got on the bed and lay flat on his back. Abigail straddled him and Tina sat on his face, facing Abigail. They formed a triangle together with Darren at the bottom. While Darren's dick was deep inside Abigail's wet pussy, his tongue was travelling back and forth between Tina's clit and her anus. Darren discovered that Tina loved getting her ass eaten, so he never stopped. As Abigail rode his dick, she and Tina locked lips, while Darren licked Tina's pussy and ass. The rhythm among them was perfect. Making them cum harmoniously was Darren's mission, but he also wanted to bust his own nut. The speed of his movement increased into Abigail's wet pussy. "Take your pussy!" Abigail screamed as she started grinding harder on his dick. Tina's mouth found Abigail's breasts. The feeling was too tense for Abigail to bear. She couldn't contain her nut. "Oh shit, I'm about to cum. Make me cum," she begged. Tina reached down to rub her clit. Darren placed his tongue on Tina's clit and added pressure, while motioning it in a circle. "I'm cumming too, baby" Tina shouted out. Abigail's started shaking along with Tina as the two of them came on top of Darren. Soon Darren is heard screaming, "Here it comes!" Abigail quickly jumped off his dick and landed her mouth on it, just in time suck his semen out of his dick. Tina joined in and sucked the remnants out of Darren's dick. That night marked the first time Darren, Tina and Abigail had a threesome. They never looked back.

Chapter 40

The dynamics of Tina and Darren's marriage took a different turn when Abigail was brought into the fold. Though Tina had rejected all of the societal standards a long time ago, she still needed to face those people who held her up to those standards, her parents. Darren was all about keeping his wife happy, but in the process, he found a little more happiness of his own. They opened the door to something that they never even conveyed in their minds, but for the love of everyone involved, they were more than open to the idea. They figured the idea of a traditional family made up of a wife and a husband was established long ago by some people who decided those standards were appropriate for them. Well, Tina, Darren and Abigail decided to establish new standards for themselves. Their new standard included a relationship with three participating partners. Abigail brought more happiness into their lives and they welcomed it with open arms. Those antiquated societal standards were a thing of the past, as far as they were concerned. Happiness was the key to Darren, Tina and Abigail's nontraditional way of life.

Had they thought about how they would forever be judged for their lifestyle? Of course, they did. It started with their parents, the people who gave them life. But none of them really gave it much thought, because they were all grown and living their own lives. What about the fact that Tina and Darren wanted to have children one day? How would they explain Abigail in their lives? They knew there was no certainty that Abigail would remain a part of their relationship indefinitely, but it was a chance they were willing to take. They discussed ways of explaining to their future children, the presence of Abigail in the home. They were willing to do whatever it took to make sure they were happy, because their happiness superseded all other prejudices and hang-ups that society may have about their relationship.

It was a difficult decision to make, but after a few months of being in a relationship with Abigail, Tina and Darren asked her to move in with them. There was no point for her to waste money paying for an apartment every month anymore. Darren's business continued to thrive with the assistance of Abigail and the loving trio looked forward to the future of their relationship.

Meanwhile, Tina, Darren and Abigail kept their parents in the dark about their relationship. Tina, especially, didn't want her dad to have a heart attack if she had to divulge her lifestyle to him. They figured in due time, everyone would figure out the type of relationship they had, and it would be a lot easier to accept. However, most people were shaking their heads at them, when all three of them attended Will's wedding and Darren openly danced with Abigail in the presence of Tina. Will thought Darren was the luckiest man in the world after Tina told him about their arrangement, but he kept mum about it. In due time, they all will be outed to their family, but until then, they planned live life their way.

Darren decided to use part of the money from his settlement to take Tina and Abigail on a much needed vacation. They travelled first-class to Kenya for a week and a half and spent another week in Ghana. It was the best time of their lives.

The End

Please enjoy these sample chapters from the book, **Meeting Ms. Right (Whip Appeal)**, by Richard Jeanty

Satisfying My Needs

Thank goodness for XXL magazine. I was getting tired of getting my groove on using Playboy magazine most of the time. Sometimes, I really had to work very hard to get an erection because the skinny white centerfolds in that magazine just did not have enough booty to get a rise out of me. In addition, the sisters, who made their way into the pages of Playboy, might as well have been white because most of them had the same type of body as the white women. Who really gets off on these skinny women, anyway? A brother needs some meat on the bone.

When XXL came on the scene, it was like a blessing from above. Although it was not considered a nude magazine, the models in there were damn near naked and they had bodies that I could identify with. There were everyday, normal looking sisters in that magazine that a brother could really appreciate. These sisters did not have to be completely naked for a brother to get an erection. Masturbating became easier for me when I bought my first copy of XXL. I signed up for my monthly subscription after I purchased my first copy. It was like clockwork after a while. My bathroom saw a lot more action thanks to that magazine.

Don't get me wrong, I am not into exploiting women in any way, but I had needs as a thirty year-old man without a girlfriend. I knew these women were posing in the magazine for their own personal reasons, but I bought the magazine for my own personal reasons as well. I could only imagine seeing Halle Berry naked so many times in front of me, and after a while, I needed more of a variety. It wasn't like I had ever seen Halle Berry completely naked anywhere, anyway. I got a glimpse of her bare breasts a couple of times briefly while watching one of her movies, and I was only able to get off on that for a little while with my remote control in hand rewinding the scene over and over. However, these sisters in XXL came in all shapes, sizes, and flavors. I could have the woman I wanted everyday of the week by flipping through a few pages. If I was going to have sex by myself, I might as well have had the variety that I wanted.

When Gabrielle Union first came on the scene, I was masturbating with my eyes closed and her in my mind almost three times a week. She filled a big void in my life for a while. She was the epitome of sexy and class to me and I imagined she and I doing things that if she was aware of she would have me put in jail. How can you blame me? She was one of the sexiest women that I had ever seen on the big screen. She did not have to reveal her naked body for my imagination to run wild. She was just as sexy fully clothed, as she probably would have been naked

Being a single man at my age did not leave me too many choices when it came to sex. My hands were my favorite girls and sometimes I had more fun with them than any other parts of my body. It should not be shocking that I masturbated to satisfy my needs because ninety five percent of married men masturbate too. I believed that fifty percent of married women masturbate and ninety five percent of single women masturbate at least once a week. I had no data to prove this, but I knew I was not the only person getting my thrill with me, myself and I.

Some people have likened me to A.C Green, the ex-player for the Los Angeles Lakers, but I was quick to tell them that if I had the opportunities he has had as an athlete; my virginity would have been history a long time ago. I was not a virgin because of religious beliefs, there was a lot more to it than that as you will find out. Besides, masturbating was the safest form of sex for me.

The Ultimate Experience

I never thought the two most beautiful women in the club would ever leave with us. Whatever Dexter must have said to them had to be amazing because we were in for one magical night. All eyes were on us, as we left the club with the women. Nikki was the finer of the two; she was brown skinned with bone straight hair down her back and a body that would put any video hoochie out of work. Maria was Puerto Rican with long curly hair and a sexy accent that could make a man melt in her hands. She had a real petite body that could take a man's imagination to places that the Lord would deem forbidden.

The smiles on the ladies' faces confirmed the fact that they were down for whatever we were planning on doing with them that night. Maria kept flirting with me; she told me that she was turned on by my shyness while we were sitting in the back seat of Dexter's BMW on the way to his house. I could see that Dexter and Nikki were getting along great. She was sensually massaging his neck as he put the pedal to the metal to get us to his place as quickly as he possibly could without crashing. Nikki was licking Dexter's neck and sticking her tongue in his ear, creating a tingling sensation that almost sent him flying off the road a couple of times. My heart was beating a mile a minute with fear. However, when Maria glided her way over to me and rolled up her mini dress pass her thighs to reveal that she was not wearing any underwear, my other head took over the fear, as it stood erected. She started groping me and my tool got harder and harder. By the time we got to Dexter's place, I had Maria's breasts in my mouth sucking on them as if I was a baby looking for milk.

We all went upstairs to Dexter's pad and at the girls' suggestion; we started playing "Truth or Dare." I could not recall anyone who took more than one truth, but the dares were coming out of the woodwork. By the time we came around to Dexter the second time for a dare, we were all butt naked ready to start an orgy that was out of this world. At first, I was a little uncomfortable getting naked in front of Dexter because as cocky as he was, I thought he was packing twelve inches or something. I did not want to get embarrassed in front of the girls. However, when I saw his eight inches dangling like a ripe banana in front of the two women who seemed too eager to take a bite, I pulled off my underwear exposing my nine-inches for the ladies to salivate over. Not that it made a difference that I was slightly bigger than Dexter was, but it gave me a lot of confidence.

All four of us were sitting butt naked in Dexter's living room with a couple of hard and erected bananas ready to take part in a banana split and a couple set of tits waiting to be caressed. We were waiting for Maria to take the next dare, as it was her turn. It was as if the ladies had planned the whole thing. Nikki double dared Maria to deep-throat my nine-incher without gagging on it. And that she did. She took every inch very slowly in her mouth and by the time the head of my penis reached the back of her throat, it felt like I was hitting her sugar walls. The look on Maria's face alone as she slowly deep throat all of me, must've sent enough blood rushing down to my meat, causing it to grow even bigger. The fact that she was massaging my balls as she took me in her mouth almost caused me to have one of those quick orgasms and embarrass myself in front of everyone.

Maria went to pull my Kielbasa out of her mouth and Nikki ordered her to keep it there until she said otherwise. Nikki continued to instruct her to suck it, and that she did. While I was trying my best to keep from exploding in Maria's mouth, it was Dexter's turn to take a dare and Nikki dared him to penetrate Maria from behind. Without hesitation, Dexter wrapped his "Grade A" beef in a condom, inserted it inside Maria and slowly started stroking her from the back while she juggled my nuts in her mouth as I stood in front of her. Nikki was a spectator for all but five minutes while Maria tried to take us both on.

Nikki's turn to take a dare had finally arrived and I dared her to stand on the couch and stick her ass up to Dexter's face so he could eat her while stroking Maria. It seemed like Nikki could not wait to be eaten. She jumped on Dexter's leather couch still wearing her heels and stuck her ass up as high as she could near his face without falling over. It was almost awkward; somehow, she managed to get in the right position for Dexter to stick his tongue in and out of her. He ate her out until she started shaking in a trance while he was still stroking the hell out of Maria. All I could hear was the moaning and groaning of the two women.

By the time Dexter and I switched positions with the two women, we had ignored the fact that we were playing

"Truth or Dare" it had become a free-for-all orgy. I could not wait to pick up Maria's little ass and start banging her around the room. She jumped on me like a little kid who had not seen her father in years. She wrapped her legs around my body as she took all my nine inches inside of her in the middle of Dexter's living room. After about ten minutes of stroking her with all my might, I laid her down on her knees on the chair and started banging her from behind.

I could see Dexter on the other side of the room with Nikki's ass hanging upside down swallowing him whole while he ate

her to ecstasy with her legs wrapped around his shoulders. Dexter appeared to be an oral expert from all the moaning that Nikki was doing. Nikki got me turned on even more and I wanted to get a piece of her as well. Therefore, I picked up Maria's little ass while still inside of her and brought her over to the other side near Dexter and Nikki. Dexter sat on the couch as the two women stood with their asses sticking up in the air sucking him off. I grabbed a hold of Nikki's ass and slowly penetrated her from behind and inserted a couple of fingers inside Maria. I developed a rhythm that was both Latin and R & B the way I was pleasing these women. By the time I was ready to climax, my phone rang and it was Dexter calling to see if I wanted to hang out with him later that evening.

I woke up almost drowning in my own semen and sweat like I had just run a marathon. It was weird for me to talk to Dexter in my position, so I told him I would call him later. I had a long day at work earlier that Friday and I came home and dozed off. Other than beating my meat, my wet dreams was the only other way I ever got my thrills and someone seemed to always interrupt my flow with a phone call.

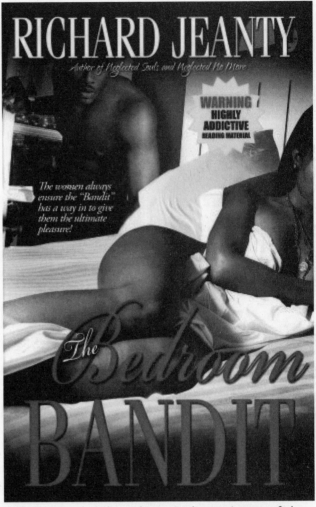

It may not be Wysteria Lane, but these desperate housewives are fed up with their neglecting husbands. Their sexual needs take precedence over the millions of dollars their husbands bring home every year to keep them happy in their affluent neighborhood. Is the bandit swift enough to evade these angry husbands?

In Stores!!

NEGLECTED SOULS

Motherhood and the trials of loving too hard and not enough frame this story...The realism of these characters will bring tears to your spirit as you discover the hero in the villain you never saw coming...

In Stores!!!

Jimmy and Nina continue to feel a void in their lives because they haven't a clue about their genealogical make-up. Jimmy falls victims to a life threatening illness and only the right organ donor can save his life. Will the donor be the bridge to reconnect Jimmy and Nina to their biological family? Will Nina be the strength for her brother in his time of need? Will they ever find out what really happened to their mother?

In Stores!!!

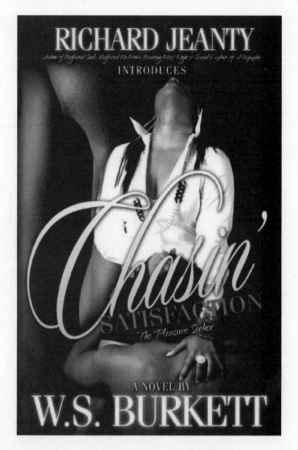

Betrayal, lust, lies, murder, deception, sex and tainted love frame this story... Julian Stevens lacks the ambition and freak ability that Miko looks for in a man, but she married him despite his flaws to spite an ex-boyfriend. When Miko least expects it, the old boyfriend shows up and ready to sweep her off her feet again. She wants to have her cake and eat it too. While Miko's doing her own thing, Julian is determined to become everything Miko ever wanted in a man and more, but will he go to extreme lengths to prove he's worthy of Miko's love? Julian Stevens soon finds out that he's capable of being more than he could ever imagine as he embarks on a journey that will change his life forever.

In Stores!!!

The police in New York and other major cities around the country are increasingly victimizing black men. The violence has escalated to deadly force, most of the time without justification. In this controversial book, noted author Richard Jeanty, tackles the problem of police brutality and the unfair treatment of Black men at the hands of police in New York City and the rest of the country.

In Stores!!!

Just when Darren thinks his relationship with Tina is flourishing, there is yet another hurdle on the road hindering their bliss. Tina saw a therapist for months to deal with her sexual addiction, but now Darren is wondering if she was ever treated completely. Darren has not been taking care of home and Tina's frustrated and agrees to a break-up with Darren. Will Darren lose Tina for good? Will Tina ever realize that Darren is the best man for her?

In Stores!!

Ronald Murphy was a player all his life until he and his best friend, Myles, met the women of their dreams during a brief vacation in South Beach, Florida. Sexual Jeopardy is story of trust, betrayal, forgiveness, friendship and hope.
In Stores!!!

Tina develops an insatiable sexual appetite very early in life. She only loves her boyfriend, Darren, but he's too far away in college to satisfy her sexual needs.
Tina decides to get buck wild away in college
Will her sexual trysts jeopardize the lives of the men in her life?

In Stores!!!

Faith Jones, a woman in her mid-thirties, has given up on ever finding love again until she met her son's best friend, Darius. Faith Jones is walking a thin line of betrayal against her son for the love of Darius. Will Faith allow her emotions to outweigh her common sense?

In Stores!!!

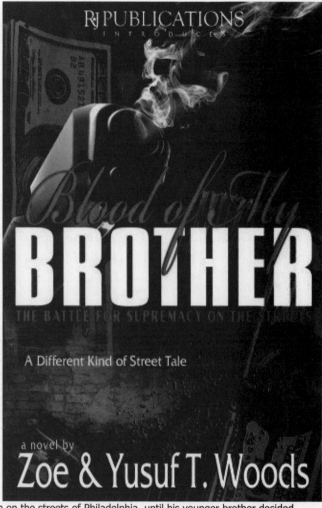

Roc was the man on the streets of Philadelphia, until his younger brother decided it was time to become his own man by wreaking havoc on Roc's crew without any regards for the blood relation they share. Drug, murder, mayhem and the pursuit of happiness can lead to deadly consequences. This story can only be told by a person who has lived it.
In Stores!!!

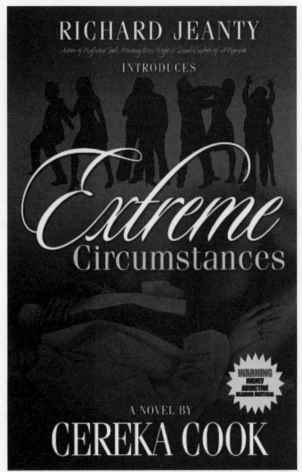

What happens when a devoted woman is betrayed? Come take a ride with Chanel as she takes her boyfriend, Donnell, to circumstances beyond belief after he betrays her trust with his endless infidelities. How long can Chanel's friend, Janai, use her looks to get what she wants from men before it catches up to her? Find out as Janai's gold-digging ways catch up with and she has to face the consequences of her extreme actions.

In Stores!!!

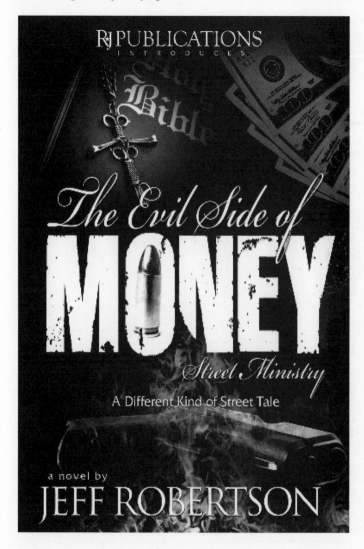

Violence, Intimidation and carnage are the order as Nathan and his brother set out to build the most powerful drug empires in Chicago. However, when God comes knocking, Nathan's conscience starts to surface. Will his haunted criminal past get the best of him?

Out of Stock until 5/15/13

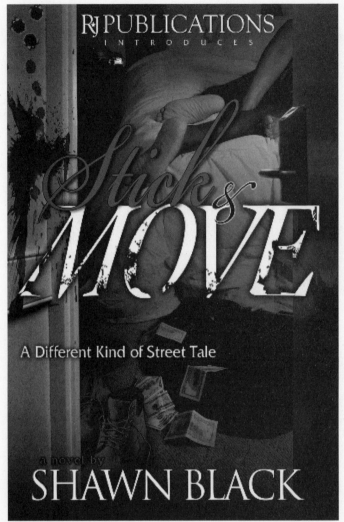

Yasmina witnessed the brutal murder of her parents at a young age at the hand of a drug dealer. This event stained her mind and upbringing as a result. Will Yamina's life come full circle with her past? Find out as Yasmina's crew, The Platinum Chicks, set out to make a name for themselves on the street.

In stores!!

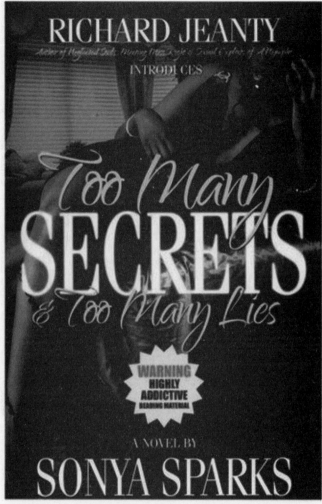

Ashland's mother, Bianca, fights hard to suppress the truth from her daughter because she doesn't want her to marry Jordan, the grandson of an ex-lover she loathes. Ashland soon finds out how cruel and vengeful her mother can be, but what price will Bianca pay for redemption?

In stores!!

Malcolm is a wealthy virgin who decides to conceal his wealth
From the world until he meets the right woman. His wealthy best friend, Dexter, hides his wealth from no one. Malcolm struggles to find love in an environment where vanity and materialism are rampant, while Dexter is getting more than enough of his share of women. Malcolm needs develop self-esteem and confidence to meet the right woman and Dexter's confidence is borderline arrogance.
Will bad boys like Dexter continue to take women for a ride?
Or will nice guys like Malcolm continue to finish last?

In Stores!!!

What happens when a woman's devotion to her fiancee is tested weeks before she gets married? What if her fiancee is just hiding behind the veil of ministry to deceive her? Find out as Sean Mitchell takes you on a journey you'll never forget into the lives of Angelica, Titus and Aurelius.

In Stores!!

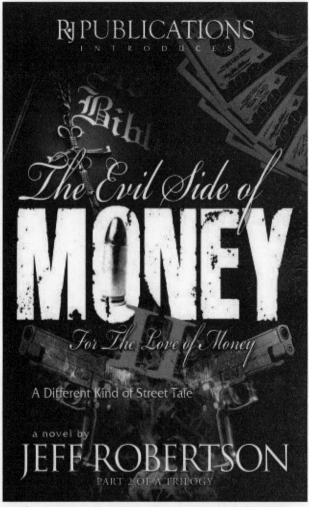

A beautigul woman from Bolivia threatens the existence of the drug empire that Nate and G have built. While Nate is head over heels for her, G can see right through her. As she brings on more conflict between the crew, G sets out to show Nate exactly who she is before she brings about their demise.

Out of stock until 5/15/13

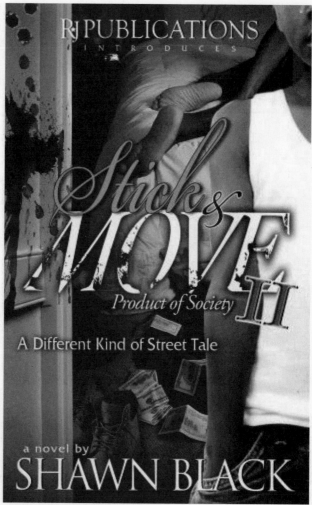

Scorcher and Yasmina's low key lifestyle was interrupted when they were taken down by the Feds, but their daughter, Serosa, was left to be raised by the foster care system. Will Serosa become a product of her environment or will she rise above it all? Her bloodline is undeniable, but will she be able to control it?

In Stores!!

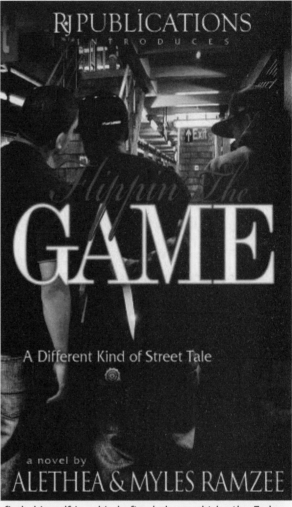

An ex-drug dealer finds himself in a bind after he's caught by the Feds. He has to decide which is more important, his family or his loyalty to the game. As he fights hard to make a decision, those who helped him to the top fear the worse from him. Will he get the chance to tell the govt. whole story, or will someone get to him before he becomes a snitch?

Out of stock until 5/15/13

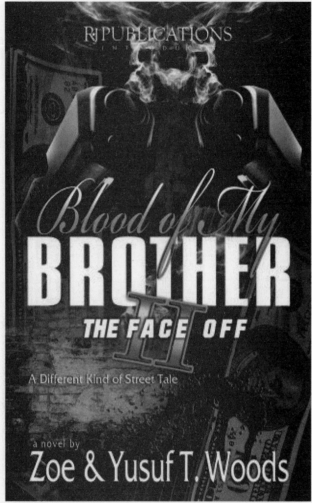

What will Roc do when he finds out the true identity of Solo? Will the blood shed come from his own brother Lil Mac? Will Roc and Solo take their beef to an explosive height on the street? Find out as Zoe and Yusuf bring the second installment to their hot street joint, Blood of My Brother.

In Stores!!!

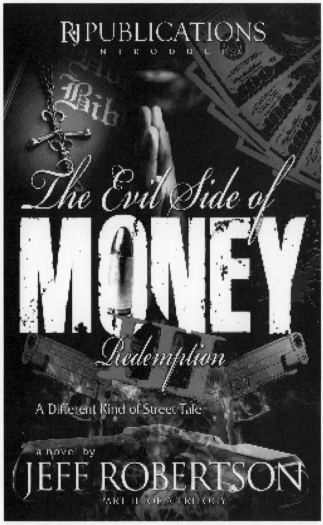

Forced to abandon the drug world for good, Nathan and G attempt to change their lives and move forward, but will their past come back to haunt them? This final installment will leave you speechless.

In Stores!!!

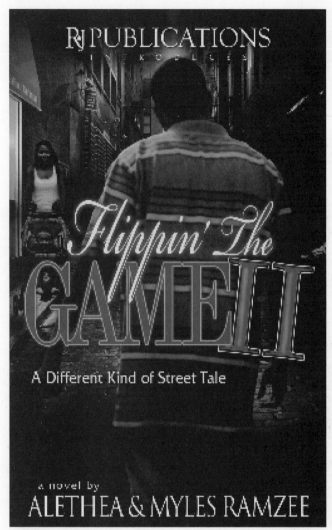

Nafys Muhammad managed to beat the charges in court, but will he beat them on the street? There will be many revelations in this story as betrayal, greed, sex scandal corruption and murder unravels throughout every page. Get ready for a rough ride.

In Stores!!!

Deon is at the mercy of a ruthless gang that kidnapped him. In a foreign land where he knows nothing about the culture, he has to use his survival instincts and his wit to outsmart his captors. Will the Hoodfellas show up in time to rescue Deon, or will Crazy D take over once again and fight an all out war by himself?

In Stores!!!

While Yasmina sits on death row awaiting her fate, her daughter, Serosa, is fighting the fight of her life on the outside. Her genetic structure that indirectly bins her to her parents could also be her downfall and force her to see that there's no way out!

In Stores!!!

The drama continues as Deshun is hunted by Angela who still feels that ex-girlfriend Kayla is still trying to win his heart, though he brutally raped her. Angela will kill anyone who gets in her way, but is DeShun worth all the aggravation?

In Stores!!!

Buck Johnson was forced to make the best out of worst situation. He has
witnessed the most cruel events in his life and it is those events who the
man that he has become. Was the Johnson family ignorant souls through
no fault of their own?

In Stores!

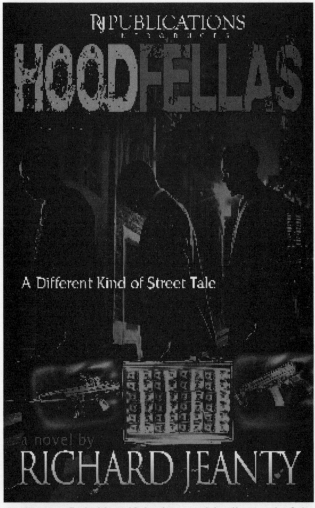

When an Ex-con finds himself destitute and in dire need of the basic necessities after he's released from prison, he turns to what he knows best, crime, but at what cost? Extortion, murder and mayhem drives him back to the top, but will he stay there?

In Stores !!!

What happens when someone falls insanely in love? Stalking is just the beginning.
In Stores!!!

My Partner's Wife

In this twisted tale of seduction, Marcus Williams finds himself taking refuge in the arms of a woman completely forbidden to him after he discovered his cheating fiancee s sexual trysts. His life spirals out of control after the death of his partner while the killer is still on the loose. Marcus is conflicted about his decision to honor his partner or to completely allow his heart to decide his fate. Always the sucker for love, Marcus starts to fall head over heels for his partner s wife. However, with more deaths on the horizon, Marcus may soon find himself serving time with the same convicts he had been putting behind bars.

In Stores!!!

Deceived I, II, III

Rhasan Jones was given a second chance at life when he moved from his slum ridden North Carolina neighborhood to Newport News, VA to live with his grandparents. It didn't take long for him to figure out all the ghettos in America were just the same. After being introduced to a crack epidemic sweeping the nation, he met Cross, a crazed New Yorker who would stop at nothing for his thirst for life's finer things...

In Stores!!!

Going all Out I, II & III

When Pharoah megtg Tez, he thought he was helping by putting him on. But he never anticipated that tez would turn to a lunatic. A blood thirty dude, Tez kills at will with no regard for life and no one is off limits. Pharoah now has to watch his back because Tez is out of control...

In Stores!!!

Hoodfellas III

Deon and his crew are forced to return back to the States. However, lurking in Deon's mind is revenge for the death of his fallen crewmembers. This personal vendetta has to be settled before Deon and the Hoodfellas can have peace of mind, but at what price will revenge come?

In Stores!!!

Use this coupon to order by mail

1. Neglected Souls, Richard Jeanty $14.95 Available
2. Neglected No More, Richard Jeanty $14.95 Avail
3. Ignorant Souls, Richard Jeanty $15.00, Available
4. Sexual Exploits of Nympho, Richard Jeanty $14.95 Available
5. Meeting Ms. Right's Whip Appeal, Richard Jeanty $14.95
6. Me and Mrs. Jones, K.M Thompson $14.95Available
7. Chasin' Satisfaction, W.S Burkett $14.95 Available
8. Extreme Circumstances, Cereka Cook $14.95 Available
9. The Most Dangerous Gang In America, R. Jeanty $15.00 Avail.
10. Sexual Exploits of a Nympho II, Richard Jeanty $15.00 Avail.
11. Sexual Jeopardy, Richard Jeanty $14.95 Available
12. Too Many Secrets, Too Many Lies, Sonya Sparks $15.00 Avail
13. Too Many Secrets, Too Many Lies II, S. Sparks, $15.00 Available
14. Stick And Move, Shawn Black $15.00 Available
15. Evil Side Of Money, Jeff Robertson $15.00 out of stock til 5/15/13
16. Evil Side Of Money II, Jeff Robertson $15.00 out of stock til 5/15/13
17. Evil Side Of Money III, Jeff Robertson $15.00Available
18. Flippin' The Game, Alethea and M. Ramzee, $15.00 out of stock til 5/15/13
19. Flippin' The Game II, Alethea and M. Ramzee, $15.00 Available
20. Cater To Her, W.S Burkett $15.00 Available
21. Blood of My Brother I, Zoe & Yusuf Woods $15.00 Avail.
22. Blood of my Brother II, Zoe & Yusuf Woods $15.00 Avail.
23. Blood of My Brother III, Zoe & Yusuf Woods $15.00 Avail.
24. Hoodfellas, Richard Jeanty $15.00 available
25. Hoodfellas II, Richard Jeanty, $15.00 Available
26. Hoodfellas III, Richard Jeanty, $15.00 Avail
27. Bedroom Bandit, Richard Jeanty $15.00 Out of Stock til 5/15/13
28. Mr. Erotica, Richard Jeanty, $15.00, Available
29. Stick N Move I, Shawn Black, $15.00 Available
30. Stick N Move II, Shawn Black $15.00 Available
31. Stick N Move III, Shawn Black $15.00 Available
32. Miami Noire, W.S. Burkett $15.00 Available
33. Insanely In Love, Cereka Cook $15.00 Available
34. My partner's wife 11/2010
35. Deceived I, The Phantom $15.00 Available
36. Deceived II, The Phantom, $15.00 Available
37. Deceived III, The Phantom, $15.00 Available
38. Going All Out I, Dorian Sykes, $15.00 Available
39. Going All Out II, Dorian Sykes, $15.00 Available

40. Going All Out III, Dorian Sykes, $15.00 Available
41. King of Detroit, Dorian Sykes, $15.00, Available
42.

Name_____

Address_____
City_____State_____Zip Code_____

Please send novels circled above; Shipping and Handling: Free
Total Number of Books_____
Tax $1.50 per book_____
Total Amount Due_____

Buy 3 books and get 1 free. Allow 2-3 weeks for delivery
Send institution check or money order only (no cash, personal check, or CODs) to:
RJ Publications
PO Box 300310
Jamaica, NY 11434

Use this coupon to order by mail
1.   Neglected Souls, Richard Jeanty $14.95 Available
2.   Neglected No More, Richard Jeanty $14.95 Avail
3.   Ignorant Souls, Richard Jeanty $15.00, Available
4.   Sexual Exploits of Nympho, Richard Jeanty $14.95 Available
5.   Meeting Ms. Right's Whip Appeal, Richard Jeanty $14.95
6.   Me and Mrs. Jones, K.M Thompson $14.95Available
7.   Chasin' Satisfaction, W.S Burkett $14.95 Available
8.   Extreme Circumstances, Cereka Cook $14.95 Available
9.   The Most Dangerous Gang In America, R. Jeanty $15.00 Avail.
10. Sexual Exploits of a Nympho II, Richard Jeanty $15.00 Avail.
11. Sexual Jeopardy, Richard Jeanty $14.95 Available
12. Too Many Secrets, Too Many Lies, Sonya Sparks $15.00 Avail
13. Too Many Secrets, Too Many Lies II, S. Sparks, $15.00 Available
14. Stick And Move, Shawn Black $15.00 Available
15. Evil Side Of Money, Jeff Robertson $15.00 out of stock til 5/15/13
16. Evil Side Of Money II, Jeff Robertson $15.00 out of stock til 5/15/13
17. Evil Side Of Money III, Jeff Robertson $15.00Available
18. Flippin' The Game, Alethea and M. Ramzee, $15.00 out of stock til 5/15/13
19. Flippin' The Game II, Alethea and M. Ramzee, $15.00 Available
20. Cater To Her, W.S Burkett $15.00 Available
21. Blood of My Brother I, Zoe & Yusuf Woods $15.00 Avail.
22. Blood of my Brother II, Zoe & Yusuf Woods $15.00 Avail.
23. Blood of My Brother III, Zoe & Yusuf Woods $15.00 Avail.
24. Hoodfellas, Richard Jeanty $15.00 available
25. Hoodfellas II, Richard Jeanty, $15.00 Available
26. Hoodfellas III, Richard Jeanty, $15.00 Avail
27.   Bedroom Bandit, Richard Jeanty $15.00 Out of Stock til 5/15/13
28. Mr. Erotica, Richard Jeanty, $15.00, Available
29. Stick N Move I, Shawn Black, $15.00 Available
30. Stick N Move II, Shawn Black $15.00 Available
31. Stick N Move III, Shawn Black $15.00 Available
32. Miami Noire, W.S. Burkett $15.00 Available
33. Insanely In Love, Cereka Cook $15.00 Available
34. My partner's wife 11/2010
35. Deceived I, The Phantom $15.00 Available
36. Deceived II, The Phantom, $15.00 Available
37. Deceived III, The Phantom, $15.00 Available
38. Going All Out I, Dorian Sykes, $15.00 Available

39. Going All Out II, Dorian Sykes, $15.00 Available
40. Going All Out III, Dorian Sykes, $15.00 Available
41. King of Detroit, Dorian Sykes, $15.00, Available
42.

     Name_____

Address_____

City_____State____Zip Code_____

Please send novels circled above; Shipping and Handling: Free
Total Number of Books_____
Tax $1.50 per book_____
Total Amount Due_____

     Buy 3 books and get 1 free. Allow 2-3 weeks for delivery

Send institution check or money order only (no cash, personal check, or CODs) to:
RJ Publications
PO Box 300310
Jamaica, NY 11434

 PUBLICATIONS
BRINGING EXCITEMENT, FUN AND JOY TO READING

Use this coupon to order by mail

1.   Neglected Souls, Richard Jeanty $14.95 Available
2.   Neglected No More, Richard Jeanty $14.95 Avail
3.   Ignorant Souls, Richard Jeanty $15.00, Available
4.   Sexual Exploits of Nympho, Richard Jeanty $14.95 Available
5.   Meeting Ms. Right's Whip Appeal, Richard Jeanty $14.95
6.   Me and Mrs. Jones, K.M Thompson $14.95Available
7.   Chasin' Satisfaction, W.S Burkett $14.95 Available
8.   Extreme Circumstances, Cereka Cook $14.95 Available
9.   The Most Dangerous Gang In America, R. Jeanty $15.00 Avail.
10. Sexual Exploits of a Nympho II, Richard Jeanty $15.00 Avail.
11. Sexual Jeopardy, Richard Jeanty $14.95 Available
12. Too Many Secrets, Too Many Lies, Sonya Sparks $15.00 Avail
13. Too Many Secrets, Too Many Lies II, S. Sparks, $15.00 Available
14. Stick And Move, Shawn Black $15.00 Available
15. Evil Side Of Money, Jeff Robertson $15.00 out of stock til 5/15/13
16. Evil Side Of Money II, Jeff Robertson $15.00 out of stock til 5/15/13
17. Evil Side Of Money III, Jeff Robertson $15.00Available
18. Flippin' The Game, Alethea and M. Ramzee, $15.00 out of stock til 5/15/13
19. Flippin' The Game II, Alethea and M. Ramzee, $15.00 Available
20. Cater To Her, W.S Burkett $15.00 Available
21. Blood of My Brother I, Zoe & Yusuf Woods $15.00 Avail.
22. Blood of my Brother II, Zoe & Yusuf Woods $15.00 Avail.
23. Blood of My Brother III, Zoe & Yusuf Woods $15.00 Avail.
24. Hoodfellas, Richard Jeanty $15.00 available
25. Hoodfellas II, Richard Jeanty, $15.00 Available
26. Hoodfellas III, Richard Jeanty, $15.00 Avail
27.   Bedroom Bandit, Richard Jeanty $15.00 Out of Stock til 5/15/13
28. Mr. Erotica, Richard Jeanty, $15.00, Available
29. Stick N Move I, Shawn Black, $15.00 Available
30. Stick N Move II, Shawn Black $15.00 Available
31. Stick N Move III, Shawn Black $15.00 Available
32. Miami Noire, W.S. Burkett $15.00 Available
33. Insanely In Love, Cereka Cook $15.00 Available
34. My partner's wife 11/2010
35. Deceived I, The Phantom $15.00 Available
36. Deceived II, The Phantom, $15.00 Available
37. Deceived III, The Phantom, $15.00 Available
38. Going All Out I, Dorian Sykes, $15.00 Available

39. Going All Out II, Dorian Sykes, $15.00 Available
40. Going All Out III, Dorian Sykes, $15.00 Available
41. King of Detroit, Dorian Sykes, $15.00, Available
42.
        Name_____
Address_____
City_____State_____Zip Code_____

Please send novels circled above; Shipping and Handling: Free
Total Number of Books_____
Tax $1.50 per book_____
Total Amount Due_____
        Buy 3 books and get 1 free. Allow 2-3 weeks for delivery
Send institution check or money order only (no cash, personal check, or CODs) to:
RJ Publications
PO Box 300310
Jamaica, NY 11434

Use this coupon to order by mail

1. Neglected Souls, Richard Jeanty $14.95 Available
2. Neglected No More, Richard Jeanty $14.95 Avail
3. Ignorant Souls, Richard Jeanty $15.00, Available
4. Sexual Exploits of Nympho, Richard Jeanty $14.95 Available
5. Meeting Ms. Right's Whip Appeal, Richard Jeanty $14.95
6. Me and Mrs. Jones, K.M Thompson $14.95Available
7. Chasin' Satisfaction, W.S Burkett $14.95 Available
8. Extreme Circumstances, Cereka Cook $14.95 Available
9. The Most Dangerous Gang In America, R. Jeanty $15.00 Avail.
10. Sexual Exploits of a Nympho II, Richard Jeanty $15.00 Avail.
11. Sexual Jeopardy, Richard Jeanty $14.95 Available
12. Too Many Secrets, Too Many Lies, Sonya Sparks $15.00 Avail
13. Too Many Secrets, Too Many Lies II, S. Sparks, $15.00 Available
14. Stick And Move, Shawn Black $15.00 Available
15. Evil Side Of Money, Jeff Robertson $15.00 out of stock til 5/15/13
16. Evil Side Of Money II, Jeff Robertson $15.00 out of stock til 5/15/13
17. Evil Side Of Money III, Jeff Robertson $15.00Available
18. Flippin' The Game, Alethea and M. Ramzee, $15.00 out of stock til 5/15/13
19. Flippin' The Game II, Alethea and M. Ramzee, $15.00 Available
20. Cater To Her, W.S Burkett $15.00 Available
21. Blood of My Brother I, Zoe & Yusuf Woods $15.00 Avail.
22. Blood of my Brother II, Zoe & Yusuf Woods $15.00 Avail.
23. Blood of My Brother III, Zoe & Yusuf Woods $15.00 Avail.
24. Hoodfellas, Richard Jeanty $15.00 available
25. Hoodfellas II, Richard Jeanty, $15.00 Available
26. Hoodfellas III, Richard Jeanty, $15.00 Avail
27. Bedroom Bandit, Richard Jeanty $15.00 Out of Stock til 5/15/13
28. Mr. Erotica, Richard Jeanty, $15.00, Available
29. Stick N Move I, Shawn Black, $15.00 Available
30. Stick N Move II, Shawn Black $15.00 Available
31. Stick N Move III, Shawn Black $15.00 Available
32. Miami Noire, W.S. Burkett $15.00 Available
33. Insanely In Love, Cereka Cook $15.00 Available
34. My partner's wife 11/2010
35. Deceived I, The Phantom $15.00 Available
36. Deceived II, The Phantom, $15.00 Available
37. Deceived III, The Phantom, $15.00 Available

38. Going All Out I, Dorian Sykes, $15.00 Available
39. Going All Out II, Dorian Sykes, $15.00 Available
40. Going All Out III, Dorian Sykes, $15.00 Available
41. King of Detroit, Dorian Sykes, $15.00, Available
42.

Name_____

Address_____

City_____State_____Zip Code_____

Please send novels circled above; Shipping and Handling: Free

Total Number of Books_____

Tax $1.50 per book_____

Total Amount Due_____

Buy 3 books and get 1 free. Allow 2-3 weeks for delivery

Send institution check or money order only (no cash, personal check, or CODs) to:

RJ Publications

PO Box 300310

Jamaica, NY 11434

PUBLICATIONS
BRINGING EXCITEMENT, FUN AND JOY TO READING

Use this coupon to order by mail

1. Neglected Souls, Richard Jeanty $14.95 Available
2. Neglected No More, Richard Jeanty $14.95 Avail
3. Ignorant Souls, Richard Jeanty $15.00, Available
4. Sexual Exploits of Nympho, Richard Jeanty $14.95 Available
5. Meeting Ms. Right's Whip Appeal, Richard Jeanty $14.95
6. Me and Mrs. Jones, K.M Thompson $14.95Available
7. Chasin' Satisfaction, W.S Burkett $14.95 Available
8. Extreme Circumstances, Cereka Cook $14.95 Available
9. The Most Dangerous Gang In America, R. Jeanty $15.00 Avail.
10. Sexual Exploits of a Nympho II, Richard Jeanty $15.00 Avail.
11. Sexual Jeopardy, Richard Jeanty $14.95 Available
12. Too Many Secrets, Too Many Lies, Sonya Sparks $15.00 Avail
13. Too Many Secrets, Too Many Lies II, S. Sparks, $15.00 Available
14. Stick And Move, Shawn Black $15.00 Available
15. Evil Side Of Money, Jeff Robertson $15.00 out of stock til 5/15/13
16. Evil Side Of Money II, Jeff Robertson $15.00 out of stock til 5/15/13
17. Evil Side Of Money III, Jeff Robertson $15.00Available
18. Flippin' The Game, Alethea and M. Ramzee, $15.00 out of stock til 5/15/13
19. Flippin' The Game II, Alethea and M. Ramzee, $15.00 Available
20. Cater To Her, W.S Burkett $15.00 Available
21. Blood of My Brother I, Zoe & Yusuf Woods $15.00 Avail.
22. Blood of my Brother II, Zoe & Yusuf Woods $15.00 Avail.
23. Blood of My Brother III, Zoe & Yusuf Woods $15.00 Avail.
24. Hoodfellas, Richard Jeanty $15.00 available
25. Hoodfellas II, Richard Jeanty, $15.00 Available
26. Hoodfellas III, Richard Jeanty, $15.00 Avail
27. Bedroom Bandit, Richard Jeanty $15.00 Out of Stock til 5/15/13
28. Mr. Erotica, Richard Jeanty, $15.00, Available
29. Stick N Move I, Shawn Black, $15.00 Available
30. Stick N Move II, Shawn Black $15.00 Available
31. Stick N Move III, Shawn Black $15.00 Available
32. Miami Noire, W.S. Burkett $15.00 Available
33. Insanely In Love, Cereka Cook $15.00 Available
34. My partner's wife 11/2010
35. Deceived I, The Phantom $15.00 Available
36. Deceived II, The Phantom, $15.00 Available
37. Deceived III, The Phantom, $15.00 Available
38. Going All Out I, Dorian Sykes, $15.00 Available
39. Going All Out II, Dorian Sykes, $15.00 Available

40. Going All Out III, Dorian Sykes, $15.00 Available
41. King of Detroit, Dorian Sykes, $15.00, Available
42.

Name_____

Address_____

City_____State_____Zip Code_____

Please send novels circled above; Shipping and Handling: Free

Total Number of Books_____

Tax $1.50 per book_____

Total Amount Due_____

Buy 3 books and get 1 free. Allow 2-3 weeks for delivery

Send institution check or money order only (no cash, personal check, or CODs) to:

RJ Publications

PO Box 300310

Jamaica, NY 11434

Use this coupon to order by mail

1. Neglected Souls, Richard Jeanty $14.95 Available
2. Neglected No More, Richard Jeanty $14.95 Avail
3. Ignorant Souls, Richard Jeanty $15.00, Available
4. Sexual Exploits of Nympho, Richard Jeanty $14.95 Available
5. Meeting Ms. Right's Whip Appeal, Richard Jeanty $14.95
6. Me and Mrs. Jones, K.M Thompson $14.95Available
7. Chasin' Satisfaction, W.S Burkett $14.95 Available
8. Extreme Circumstances, Cereka Cook $14.95 Available
9. The Most Dangerous Gang In America, R. Jeanty $15.00 Avail.
10. Sexual Exploits of a Nympho II, Richard Jeanty $15.00 Avail.
11. Sexual Jeopardy, Richard Jeanty $14.95 Available
12. Too Many Secrets, Too Many Lies, Sonya Sparks $15.00 Avail
13. Too Many Secrets, Too Many Lies II, S. Sparks, $15.00 Available
14. Stick And Move, Shawn Black $15.00 Available
15. Evil Side Of Money, Jeff Robertson $15.00 out of stock til 5/15/13
16. Evil Side Of Money II, Jeff Robertson $15.00 out of stock til 5/15/13
17. Evil Side Of Money III, Jeff Robertson $15.00Available
18. Flippin' The Game, Alethea and M. Ramzee, $15.00 out of stock til 5/15/13
19. Flippin' The Game II, Alethea and M. Ramzee, $15.00 Available
20. Cater To Her, W.S Burkett $15.00 Available
21. Blood of My Brother I, Zoe & Yusuf Woods $15.00 Avail.
22. Blood of my Brother II, Zoe & Yusuf Woods $15.00 Avail.
23. Blood of My Brother III, Zoe & Yusuf Woods $15.00 Avail.
24. Hoodfellas, Richard Jeanty $15.00 available
25. Hoodfellas II, Richard Jeanty, $15.00 Available
26. Hoodfellas III, Richard Jeanty, $15.00 Avail
27. Bedroom Bandit, Richard Jeanty $15.00 Out of Stock til 5/15/13
28. Mr. Erotica, Richard Jeanty, $15.00, Available
29. Stick N Move I, Shawn Black, $15.00 Available
30. Stick N Move II, Shawn Black $15.00 Available
31. Stick N Move III, Shawn Black $15.00 Available
32. Miami Noire, W.S. Burkett $15.00 Available
33. Insanely In Love, Cereka Cook $15.00 Available
34. My partner's wife 11/2010
35. Deceived I, The Phantom $15.00 Available
36. Deceived II, The Phantom, $15.00 Available
37. Deceived III, The Phantom, $15.00 Available
38. Going All Out I, Dorian Sykes, $15.00 Available

39.   Going All Out II, Dorian Sykes, $15.00 Available
40.   Going All Out III, Dorian Sykes, $15.00 Available
41.   King of Detroit, Dorian Sykes, $15.00, Available
42.

          Name_____

Address_____
City_____State_____Zip Code_____

Please send novels circled above; Shipping and Handling: Free
Total Number of Books_____
Tax $1.50 per book_____
Total Amount Due_____
          Buy 3 books and get 1 free. Allow 2-3 weeks for delivery
Send institution check or money order only (no cash, personal check, or CODs) to:
RJ Publications
PO Box 300310
Jamaica, NY 11434

Use this coupon to order by mail

1. Neglected Souls, Richard Jeanty $14.95 Available
2. Neglected No More, Richard Jeanty $14.95 Avail
3. Ignorant Souls, Richard Jeanty $15.00, Available
4. Sexual Exploits of Nympho, Richard Jeanty $14.95 Available
5. Meeting Ms. Right's Whip Appeal, Richard Jeanty $14.95
6. Me and Mrs. Jones, K.M Thompson $14.95Available
7. Chasin' Satisfaction, W.S Burkett $14.95 Available
8. Extreme Circumstances, Cereka Cook $14.95 Available
9. The Most Dangerous Gang In America, R. Jeanty $15.00 Avail.
10. Sexual Exploits of a Nympho II, Richard Jeanty $15.00 Avail.
11. Sexual Jeopardy, Richard Jeanty $14.95 Available
12. Too Many Secrets, Too Many Lies, Sonya Sparks $15.00 Avail
13. Too Many Secrets, Too Many Lies II, S. Sparks, $15.00 Available
14. Stick And Move, Shawn Black $15.00 Available
15. Evil Side Of Money, Jeff Robertson $15.00 out of stock til 5/15/13
16. Evil Side Of Money II, Jeff Robertson $15.00 out of stock til 5/15/13
17. Evil Side Of Money III, Jeff Robertson $15.00Available
18. Flippin' The Game, Alethea and M. Ramzee, $15.00 out of stock til 5/15/13
19. Flippin' The Game II, Alethea and M. Ramzee, $15.00 Available
20. Cater To Her, W.S Burkett $15.00 Available
21. Blood of My Brother I, Zoe & Yusuf Woods $15.00 Avail.
22. Blood of my Brother II, Zoe & Yusuf Woods $15.00 Avail.
23. Blood of My Brother III, Zoe & Yusuf Woods $15.00 Avail.
24. Hoodfellas, Richard Jeanty $15.00 available
25. Hoodfellas II, Richard Jeanty, $15.00 Available
26. Hoodfellas III, Richard Jeanty, $15.00 Avail
27. Bedroom Bandit, Richard Jeanty $15.00 Out of Stock til 5/15/13
28. Mr. Erotica, Richard Jeanty, $15.00, Available
29. Stick N Move I, Shawn Black, $15.00 Available
30. Stick N Move II, Shawn Black $15.00 Available
31. Stick N Move III, Shawn Black $15.00 Available
32. Miami Noire, W.S. Burkett $15.00 Available
33. Insanely In Love, Cereka Cook $15.00 Available
34. My partner's wife 11/2010
35. Deceived I, The Phantom $15.00 Available
36. Deceived II, The Phantom, $15.00 Available
37. Deceived III, The Phantom, $15.00 Available
38. Going All Out I, Dorian Sykes, $15.00 Available

39. Going All Out II, Dorian Sykes, $15.00 Available
40. Going All Out III, Dorian Sykes, $15.00 Available
41. King of Detroit, Dorian Sykes, $15.00, Available
42.

        Name_____
Address_____
City_____State_____Zip Code_____

Please send novels circled above; Shipping and Handling: Free
Total Number of Books_____
Tax $1.50 per book_____
Total Amount Due_____
              Buy 3 books and get 1 free. Allow 2-3 weeks for delivery
Send institution check or money order only (no cash, personal check, or CODs) to:
RJ Publications
PO Box 300310
Jamaica, NY 11434

Use this coupon to order by mail

1. Neglected Souls, Richard Jeanty $14.95 Available
2. Neglected No More, Richard Jeanty $14.95 Avail
3. Ignorant Souls, Richard Jeanty $15.00, Available
4. Sexual Exploits of Nympho, Richard Jeanty $14.95 Available
5. Meeting Ms. Right's Whip Appeal, Richard Jeanty $14.95
6. Me and Mrs. Jones, K.M Thompson $14.95Available
7. Chasin' Satisfaction, W.S Burkett $14.95 Available
8. Extreme Circumstances, Cereka Cook $14.95 Available
9. The Most Dangerous Gang In America, R. Jeanty $15.00 Avail.
10. Sexual Exploits of a Nympho II, Richard Jeanty $15.00 Avail.
11. Sexual Jeopardy, Richard Jeanty $14.95 Available
12. Too Many Secrets, Too Many Lies, Sonya Sparks $15.00 Avail
13. Too Many Secrets, Too Many Lies II, S. Sparks, $15.00 Available
14. Stick And Move, Shawn Black $15.00 Available
15. Evil Side Of Money, Jeff Robertson $15.00 out of stock til 5/15/13
16. Evil Side Of Money II, Jeff Robertson $15.00 out of stock til 5/15/13
17. Evil Side Of Money III, Jeff Robertson $15.00Available
18. Flippin' The Game, Alethea and M. Ramzee, $15.00 out of stock til 5/15/13
19. Flippin' The Game II, Alethea and M. Ramzee, $15.00 Available
20. Cater To Her, W.S Burkett $15.00 Available
21. Blood of My Brother I, Zoe & Yusuf Woods $15.00 Avail.
22. Blood of my Brother II, Zoe & Yusuf Woods $15.00 Avail.
23. Blood of My Brother III, Zoe & Yusuf Woods $15.00 Avail.
24. Hoodfellas, Richard Jeanty $15.00 available
25. Hoodfellas II, Richard Jeanty, $15.00 Available
26. Hoodfellas III, Richard Jeanty, $15.00 Avail
27. Bedroom Bandit, Richard Jeanty $15.00 Out of Stock til 5/15/13
28. Mr. Erotica, Richard Jeanty, $15.00, Available
29. Stick N Move I, Shawn Black, $15.00 Available
30. Stick N Move II, Shawn Black $15.00 Available
31. Stick N Move III, Shawn Black $15.00 Available
32. Miami Noire, W.S. Burkett $15.00 Available
33. Insanely In Love, Cereka Cook $15.00 Available
34. My partner's wife 11/2010
35. Deceived I, The Phantom $15.00 Available
36. Deceived II, The Phantom, $15.00 Available
37. Deceived III, The Phantom, $15.00 Available

38.   Going All Out I, Dorian Sykes, $15.00 Available
39.   Going All Out II, Dorian Sykes, $15.00 Available
40.   Going All Out III, Dorian Sykes, $15.00 Available
41.   King of Detroit, Dorian Sykes, $15.00, Available
42.

Name_____

Address_____

City_____State_____Zip Code_____

Please send novels circled above; Shipping and Handling: Free
Total Number of Books_____
Tax $1.50 per book_____
Total Amount Due_____
          Buy 3 books and get 1 free. Allow 2-3 weeks for delivery
Send institution check or money order only (no cash, personal check, or CODs) to:
RJ Publications
PO Box 300310
Jamaica, NY 11434